Crashing the Party

Crashing the Party

From the Bernie Sanders Campaign
to a Progressive Movement

Heather Gautney

With a Foreword by
Adolph Reed, Jr.

VERSO
London • New York

First published by Verso 2018
© Heather Gautney 2018
Foreword © Adolph Reed, Jr. 2018

1 3 5 7 9 10 8 6 4 2

Verso
UK: 6 Meard Street, London W1F 0EG
US: 20 Jay Street, Suite 1010, Brooklyn, NY 11201

versobooks.com

Verso is the imprint of New Left Books

ISBN-13: 978-1-78663-432-0
ISBN-13: 978-1-78663-433-7 (US EBK)
ISBN-13: 978-1-78663-447-4 (UK EBK)

British Library Cataloguing in Publication Data
A catalogue record for this book is available from the British Library

Library of Congress Cataloging-in-Publication Data
A catalog record for this book is available from the Library of Congress

Typeset in Fournier by MJ & N Gavan, Truro, Cornwall
Printed in the US by Maple Press

For my mother, Diane Gautney

Contents

Foreword by Adolph Reed, Jr.   ix

Acknowledgements   xxv

Introduction   1

1. Crashing the Party   13
2. The Campaign, Part 1: Democratic Socialism   41
3. The Campaign, Part 2: Identity Politics   71
4. The Convention, the General Election, and Its
   Aftermath   99

Conclusion: Campaigns End, Movements Endure   127

Notes   143

Index   169

Foreword

In the early spring of 2015, as the volume of chatter about the 2016 presidential race was increasing, I remarked to friends that my only interest in the process was that someone should remind me the day before the election to go vote for Hillary Clinton. That is how much it seemed a foregone conclusion that she would win the nomination and that we would once again be left to accept the only reason the neoliberal Democrats have offered most Americans to vote for them perhaps at least since Michael Dukakis: The Other Guy Is Worse (TOGIW). And the bases on which the other guy has been worse increasingly have had to do with the Republicans' bold acceleration into horrible reaction. The dominant wing of the Democratic Party has been no less militarist or interventionist than Republicans; has reduced women's political concerns to abortion rights while even in that have forsaken principled commitment to reproductive rights for women in favor of a wan, focus-group tested support for "choice"; has limited concern with inequality largely to support for antidiscrimination and the sharply class-skewed celebration of diversity; has abetted, if not driven, the national attack on public education by corporate plunderers and their 501(c)(3) shock troops; and has all but openly expressed contempt for the working class of any race, gender, or sexual orientation.

Of course, spreading the idea that Clinton's nomination was inevitable was part of her campaign strategy and has been a feature of Clintonism since Bill ran in 1992. Ever since she lost in 2008 to Obama, her supporters had laced that Clintonite entitlement with bourgeois feminism: it was her turn, many insisted, because the historic nomination of the first black president should be followed by the equally historic nomination of the first female president, as though that had been an implicit understanding on which the party united around Obama. Moreover, her supporters contended, she was on paper the most qualified candidate, based on the range and extent of prior government experience, educational attainment, and general wonkishness—in other words, her résumé of accomplishments rather than any compelling political vision.[1] That she is also, for good as well as terrible reasons, one of the most thoroughly and intensely disliked women in public life was ignored or met with the equivalent of covering one's ears and screaming, "Sexist! Sexist! Sexist!" It was clear from the first as well that her campaign would offer nothing more than TOGIW to labor and liberal-left constituencies. It depended on gender celebration, "Lean In" feminism, and Republican misogyny to mobilize "women" as an abstract demographic category, and a combination of TOGIW and friend-of-the-people-of-color posturing for the black, Latino, and other nonwhite voters. In retrospect, if not in prospect, it was clear that her candidacy and campaign brought together nearly everything that is inadequate, unsatisfying, and loathsome about the dominant wing of the Democratic Party from the standpoint of working people's concerns and Left political interests.

In that context, the news that Bernie Sanders was considering entering the race for the nomination was noteworthy; he had always been a consistent voice on the left wing of Congress. As the focus of his campaign took shape over late spring and summer, it showed potential to assert a clear critique and program centering working people's interests and concerns in the primary process. The Sanders campaign seemed to constitute a flashpoint to help galvanize labor and Left forces that have been dissatisfied for decades with the Democrats' neoliberal presumptions about the horizon of the possible; it could be a significant step toward building the working-class-based, institutionally grounded political voice necessary to disrupt the nearly forty-year, increasingly bipartisan commitment to the primacy of corporate and financial sector interests and a regime of steadily intensifying upward redistribution. Formation of the Labor for Bernie group also attested to that potential.

From that point the story is well known. Few of those active in the campaign early on were convinced that Sanders had better than a puncher's chance to win the nomination, although many thought that he was a better bet to win in November than to win the nomination. To wit, in late fall

Labor for Bernie scheduled its first large public meeting for April 1, 2016, on the assumption that the campaign would most likely be over by then, so that it would have been a good occasion to discuss next steps. Instead, the campaign was still very much alive at that date, and even those who had more modest expectations wondered how far it could go. The meeting focused mainly on ways to mobilize for coming primaries and to do whatever needed to be done to keep it alive for as long as possible.

One of the most intriguing facets of the Sanders effort was its innovative attempt to use a national election campaign to support and stimulate a movement-building project, because the two operate off quite different, in fact opposing, logics. Electoral action is all about mobilizing and connecting with existing constituencies—which means in practical terms addressing people who understand themselves more or less consciously as motivated around a given set of issues parsed and articulated in familiar ways. A serious electoral campaign, despite what many nominal leftists like to believe, must have as its paramount concern aggregating the greatest number of votes possible. At the most mundane level of door-knocking outreach, that translates into a warrant to resist tarrying in conversation with voters; the goal is to cover as much targeted territory and drop as much candidate literature as possible. The electoral imperative also impels toward formulating a message that communicates as widely as possible, favoring condensation symbols that evoke affective states over specific programs. In that sense electoral action can be more effective for demonstrating power that has already been won on the plane of social movement organizing than about movement building.

By contrast, organizing operates within a longer, less urgent, and more open-ended time horizon. Its objective is to build relationships of standing, which requires patient, intensive face-to-face interaction over time.[2] The organizing approach assumes a need to generate a base of support or constituency for a political program, not that one already exists and needs only to be mobilized; it is the approach necessary for an insurgent political project seriously focused on altering the conventional terms of debate. Sanders's campaign rode the tensions between those two approaches very effectively: he located a discourse frame and message that resonated broadly among the working-class population. (I define "working class" in line with Michael Zweig's simple criterion—those who take rather than give orders at work[3]—which includes many who are routinely characterized as middle class by virtue, for example, of homeownership or white-collar employment.) Sanders showed in dramatic fashion what some on the Left have insisted for a long time, that very many Americans of all races, genders, and sexual orientations feel that their concerns, worries, and aspirations are ignored by both political parties and that they will respond affirmatively to voices that do attempt to connect with them.

For fifteen years or more I was part of an effort to build an independent Labor Party that rested on precisely that conviction. Our last major undertaking was a successful campaign to win an official ballot line for a South Carolina Labor Party. We selected South Carolina because we had a solid base of support in the state's labor movement (the South Carolina AFL-CIO was one of our affiliates and its president, Donna Dewitt, was one of our national party co-chairs) and thick social movement connections in the state. Moreover, we thought that our success there, one of the reddest states in the country, where reactionary political forces dominated, would buttress the argument that working people anywhere would support a working-class political vision and program, if it were presented to and discussed with them directly one on one and in small group settings.[4] To that extent our effort was directed in part toward those in the institutional labor movement and elsewhere who insisted that American working people would not respond to direct class appeals. If working-class South Carolinians responded favorably, we assumed, that might help counter the hesitance that we attributed to more or less opportunistic or demoralized inclinations to underestimate the working class. We succeeded; more than 16,500 registered voters in the state, the vast majority of them working people, officially recorded support for recognition of a South Carolina Labor Party to articulate and advance an agenda important to them.

Our success in South Carolina did not sway enough skeptics in the labor movement to disrupt the inertial practice of backing corporate Democrats and hoping for the best. However, it did validate the conviction that was a cornerstone of the Labor Party experience, that working people by and large recognize that neither Democrats nor Republicans address their fundamental concerns—stable employment that provides a decent living standard and economic security and a modicum of dignity on the job, access to education, housing, health care, dignity and security in old age, and so on—and often approach the electoral realm as a domain for selecting the less bad. From that perspective, it is worth noting that of the six national unions that endorsed the Sanders campaign and Our Revolution, three—the United Electrical, Radio and Machine Workers of America; National Nurses United/California Nurses Association; and the International Longshore and Warehouse Union—were founding affiliates of the Labor Party, and the presidents of two others, the Amalgamated Transit Union and American Postal Workers Union, were active Labor Party members and leaders. The Sanders campaign rested on similar convictions regarding the potential for an openly working-class-based political program to resonate widely within the general population.

No matter how much its early achievements stoked enthusiasm, the Sanders campaign was always a long shot to win the nomination. The campaign's success in navigating tensions between electoral and movement-building logics obscured its long shot character for a time, but the odds always were much greater that Clinton would be the eventual nominee. It is important to keep that in mind because a fundamentally counterproductive discussion of why Sanders failed to win the nomination gained currency in the campaign's wake. Much of that discussion is Monday morning quarterbacking, a stalking horse for assertions that, if the campaign had followed some other trajectory favored by those making the claims, it would have been more successful, or an implication that not having won the nomination renders the effort retrospectively to have been misguided or a waste of time. The important questions concern not why Sanders "failed" but how we should approach going forward to build on the momentum the campaign generated. This is a reason that *Crashing the Party* is an important political intervention. Gautney's account of the campaign not only has the virtues of an insider's knowledge and perspective; it is also focused on how to understand and build on the momentum the campaign generated.

How to think about and approach going forward is the key. As I write three months into the Trump presidency, the internet- and identity-based Left is by and large doing what it does—issuing and squabbling over grand pronouncements, as often as not onanistically self-indulgent; rooting around for putative evidence of a sellout and expatiating on whether "we" should align with corporate Democrats or Democrats at all as a question of high principle; urging cautions or hurling accusations, commonly driven by anachronistic analogies, about capitulating to racism and sexism within the white working class and self-righteously rehearsing poll data purported to prove that those were white workers' essential motivations for voting for Trump; and spinning off into affront-seeking ersatz politics such as mobilizing against ads for Pepsi and shea butter. One might have thought that Trump's election would have a bracing effect against persisting in such pointless and counter-productive idiocies. For some who frequent that ersatz left world it has; for many others, however, the election and its likely consequences have not led to critical reflection, and for all too many it has led to doubling down on the interpretive pathologies that have deepened its irrelevance over the past generation. It would be wise to recall that reality as we filter through the skeins of breathless controversy over one or another blog posting or Twitter war.

Clintonoid liberals have their own narratives that minimize the lessons to be drawn from Trump's victory. Those mainly ring changes on familiar excuses: the "we really won, but they stole it" line goes back to Gore and Kerry. (Republicans cheated in all three races, to be sure, but none should have been close enough—Bush was a dog of a candidate in 2000, more so in 2004, and Trump is Trump—for GOP shenanigans to have turned the election.) Or that Nader created confusion and made them look bad and weakened them unfairly in 2000, and Sanders did the same in 2016. What stands out about that line in particular is its implication that mainstream Democrats have a right to every left of center vote without having to do anything to earn it. That view is consistent with their conviction that there can be no realistic alternative to a politics centered on Wall Street and the investor class and that it is naïve and irresponsibly utopian to imagine otherwise. Clintonoids commonly attributed Kerry's defeat to the backwardness and bigotry of white working-class voters. As an (African American) Ivy League colleague said to me only days after the 2004 election, in rebuffing my suggestions of reasons such voters in economically depressed areas might have had to be skeptical about Kerry, "You have to admit, Adolph, those people just aren't like us," by which she meant that they were benighted, small-minded bigots. Between 2008 and 2016 that smug perception became a foundational premise of Democratic neoliberalism. It meshes seamlessly with their disdain for public institutions, their insistence that poor people "play by the rules" and that Hillary Clinton's infamous "basket of deplorables" comment has been criticized unfairly as a castigation of Trump voters across the board, whereas she intended it as a reference to the genuinely deplorable pack of crypto-fascist, racist, and misogynist elements that flocked to his campaign. However, she was vulnerable to that misreading because the Clintonoid wing of the party—including her, Obama, and Bill Clinton—has catered so conspicuously to the investor class and professional-managerial strata. Trump's nomination only gave her an excuse to target her campaign to the "moderate Republicans" who exist mainly in pollsters' heads; she almost certainly would have done so anyway.

The 2016 election's outcome underscored Labor Party founder Anthony Mazzocchi's sober warning, after his noting that the Democrats offer little to address the worsening insecurity among the broad working class, that unless labor and the Left offer a compelling political and programmatic alternative, dangerously reactionary forces could make major inroads among working people by providing superficially plausible diagnoses and programs driven by scapegoating and repression.[5] And here we are.

Crashing the Party articulates a perspective that points toward how we might build on the excitement and momentum the Sanders campaign generated. That is especially important now that reactionaries control the federal government as well as thirty-three governorships and twenty-five state legislatures. The key objectives are straightforward. We need to focus on taking back as many state legislatures, governorships, and congressional seats from Republicans as we possibly can in 2018. That is both a defensive and an offensive objective. The paramount imperative is to block and slow the right-wing juggernaut in whatever ways and on whatever fronts we can because those forces are intent on destroying every bit of social protection won during the past hundred years or more. That focus on the immediate task would also feed efforts to create space for and build toward doing more in 2020 and beyond. That objective will require connecting with people—including as many Trump voters as possible—who do not automatically identify as liberals or progressives around concerns that are shared broadly and issues that sharpen the contradictions within the Trump/GOP electoral base, particularly among those working people who have become part of that base by default because Democratic neoliberalism offers them so little.

It should also be clear that the patterns of political alliance and mobilization with which we have been operating are not sufficiently effective. In part this is because, as the Democrats' center of gravity has moved rightward, the TOGIW rationale has increasingly neglected or even sacrificed the concerns of the working-class base to demonstrate political maturity or responsibility—that is, to satisfy Wall Street.

Recent Illinois governor Pat Quinn is a stellar example of this strategy and where it leads. On being elected, he almost immediately went on the attack against public sector unions that had played a significant part in electing him. When he ran for re-election, he still carried the union vote against Republican hedge fund billionaire Bruce Rauner, but his percentage of union support, as well as that among other solid Democratic constituencies, fell enough to bring about his defeat and thereby deliver the state into years of horror. One can argue that Quinn's and Clinton's campaigns were flawed, incoherent, and chaotic internally, but all campaigns are; the fact remains that Rauner's election in 2014 and Trump's in 2016 are culminations of the TOGIW strategy.

Barack Obama's successes in 2008 and 2012 fed the impression that Democrats could win with an electoral coalition based on a redefined liberalism centered on ascriptively defined constituencies—blacks; Hispanics and other nonwhites; lesbian, gay, bisexual, transgender, queer, intersex, and allied people; women—while substituting commitment to diversity and multiculturalism within neoliberal class relations for pursuit of downward economic redistribution and counting on TOGIW to induce unions to fund and mobilize for them. As a purely electoral gambit, however, the numbers do not add up to a dependable electoral majority. Obama's initial victory was assisted by the novelty effect of the possibility of a first black presidency, which boosted turnout and seemed to offer some affirmative reason to vote instead of just TOGIW, and the economic crash also primed voters for a message of generic "change." Clinton's candidacy in 2016 did not generate the same enthusiasm, even as her minions and running dogs tried to stress the historic significance of electing the first woman president. Sexism no doubt played a part, and, despite her apparatus's constant complaint that she should win as the best qualified, she was a damaged candidate from the start. In addition, eight years of an Obama presidency that did so little to follow through on the grand but evanescent promise of deliverance evoked in the mystique of his presidential First may have left many voters wary of continuing in that vein.[6]

Moreover, the decision to mobilize on those terms, while not also making appeals to working-class concerns, provided Republicans an opportunity to mobilize *against* diversity and multiculturalism in part by tying those values to populations, at the top and the bottom of the social order, that could be scapegoated as responsible for (white) working-class insecurity. In short, a crucial lesson to be taken from the Trump victory is that by skirting the concerns of working people of all races, genders, sexual orientations, and so on, Democratic neoliberalism is self-defeating and, as Tony Mazzocchi warned, paves the way for reactionaries. Holding off the Republican juggernaut will require a break from the counterproductive political strategy that aims to appeal in the same ways to the same more or less formalistic, artificial constituencies that have anchored Democratic neoliberalism's version of a social base, the same approach to coalition-building that has disdained working-class concerns to the detriment of egalitarian interests across the board. National coordinator of the Labor Campaign for Single Payer and former Labor Party leader Mark Dudzic makes the point with wonderful clarity and pungency, in an essay written just after the Democratic and Republican conventions. He notes:

> Many in the Democratic establishment blame backward white workers for the success of the Bernie Sanders insurgency. Joan Walsh, among many others, opined that Sanders' substantial support among white workers (who overwhelmingly supported Clinton in 2008) is because "she has been damaged by her association with the first black president." And Paul Krugman, that eternal guardian of the left gate of the ruling class, pontificated that the Sanders campaign failed to understand the importance of "horizontal inequality" between groups. What the fuck does that even mean? The "white working class," like the "black community," is an abstraction that does not exist anywhere in the real world. The US working class is broad and diverse. It's not even all that white any more and certainly not all that male. Its conditions are determined by its position within a political economy but, like everyone else, the experience and consciousness of individual workers is formed by a whole series of contingent relationships and experiences. The recent use of the trope of the angry white working class attempts to extract white workers from these class dynamics and present them as a demonized and marginalized natural group.[7]

It should be clear as well that elevation of questions like whether we should align with Democrats to a level of core political principle is dilettantish bullshit. The only answer to such questions can be, "It depends on particular circumstances, local political histories and patterns of alliance, and what the actual alternatives are." *Crashing the Party* can be an important resource to assist reckoning at the concrete levels at which we must focus if we are to turn the reactionary tide.

Adolph Reed, Jr.

Acknowledgements

Thanks to the American Sociological Association and the American Association for the Advancement of Science for sponsoring my US Senate fellowship and to Fordham University for its generous support.

Thanks to Jeff Weaver, Mark Longabaugh, and Brad Deutsch for the platform experience; to Bernie's platform committee and delegates, especially Dottie Deans, Diane Lanpher, and Ellen Oxfeld; to the sixty-plus people who donated an average of $29 to help get me to Orlando and Philadelphia; and to everyone in Bernie's Senate office and the budget committee.

Thanks to "Higher Ed for Bernie" friends, especially Samir Sonti, Doug Henwood, Liza Featherstone, and Les Leopold; as well as South Carolina campaigners and comrades Donna DeWitt, Robert Greene, Willie Legette, Erin McKee, Lawrence Moore, and Pat Sullivan.

Special thanks to John Halle, Bill DiFazio, Susanna

Heller, Frances Fox Piven, Akim Reinhardt, Hector Sigala, Andy Ryan, John Schoneboom, Ben St. Clair, and Alex Vitale.

And to my agent, William Clark, and my editors at Verso, Andy Hsaio and Ben Mabie.

With love and thanks to my family, Diane, Dan, Kristen, Jeff, DeeAnn, Jake, Robbie, Spencer, Jill, Joe, Olivia, Annabella, and Vittoria. And in loving memory of Spencer E. Gautney, Jr., Neil Smith, and Representative Joe Neal.

Extra special thanks to Adolph Reed, Jr., Larry Cohen, Cornel West, Warren Gunnels, John Judis, Michael Briggs, Phil Fiermonte, Sophie Kasimow, Micki McGee, Billy Gendell, Josh Hoxie, David Weinstein, and, most of all, Jane and Bernie Sanders, Glenn Kaplan, and my precious Lula and Sydney.

Introduction

This book is about Bernie Sanders's remarkable presidential campaign and the crashing of the Democratic Party in 2016. Over the course of Barack Obama's presidency, Democrats lost nearly 1,000 seats in state legislatures, in some cases to Republicans with far-right agendas.[1] In 2009, they held 257 seats in the House of Representatives. But by January 2017, that number had dwindled to 194. During that same period, they lost 12 Senate seats and more than half the governorships they held.[2] In large parts of the country, the Democratic Party continues to have no political influence at all.

Despite these abysmal trends, the Democrats overwhelmingly favored establishment candidate Hillary Clinton in 2016. She was historically unpopular, beset by repeated scandal, and fervently rejected by the party's progressive base. A democratic socialist and career Independent, Vermont senator Bernie Sanders, won nearly half of the votes in what many believe to have been a fixed primary. Despite losing, he can lay claim to record-breaking numbers among young voters and worldwide celebrity.

Then the unthinkable happened: America's soon-to-be first woman president lost the general election to billionaire reality TV star and real estate mogul Donald Trump, a political neophyte known for his extremist views and social indecency.

I worked for Bernie before his presidential campaign, though I do not go nearly as far back with him as those in his inner circle, especially those from Vermont. I served in his Washington, DC, office as a legislative fellow on leave from my university and worked on the campaign as a volunteer researcher and organizer.

I'm a university professor, not a gossip columnist, so this book does not offer coveted details on how Bernie fixes his hair or what he eats for dinner. Nor does it offer blow-by-blow reporting on the interpersonal dramas in and outside of his campaign or pay homage to the spectacular.

It is also does not claim to represent Bernie's presidential campaign in its totality. Like most national electoral endeavors, his was a complex organization with many threads, weaving together hundreds, if not thousands, of distinct people and perspectives. My account is just one of them.

What this book *does* do is offer insights from up-close work with Bernie, mixed in with historical and sociological analysis, to perform an autopsy of the 2016 election—and to reflect on how his presidential campaign transformed US politics and inspired a generation.

The first time I met Bernie Sanders was in his DC Senate office, about fifteen minutes before his weekly Friday appearance on Thom Hartmann's radio show. I was on sabbatical from Fordham University, and my research agenda was "in transition." Most of my intellectual and political work before then focused on social movements and progressive politics at the margins of state power—an outgrowth of my experience with social inequality as an adolescent in the Reagan years, that period of total defeat, when vital public services were scaled back and the portion of the nation's wealth held by the top 1 percent nearly doubled (from 22 to 39 percent).[3]

Reagan famously remarked in a news conference in 1983 that "what I want to see above all is that this country remains a country where someone can always get rich."[4] But his administration's "tightening" of eligibility requirements ushered my once middle-class family into the ranks of the poor by denying disability benefits to my father after he suffered a major stroke. Masses of recipients had their benefits similarly denied through what the Government Accountability Office found to be a botched cost-savings program. Some committed suicide. Others died trying to obtain coverage under an otherwise solvent Social Security program that Reagan and chairman of the Federal Reserve Alan Greenspan raided to pay for corporate tax cuts and defense spending.[5] My family, like many others, blamed ourselves for the stigma of poverty that conservatives propagated with their talk of personal responsibility and "welfare queens."[6] That is the experience that Bernie has sought to eradicate. Above all, he wants the United States to become a country where no one can be poor.

Despite my early education on inequality in America, it was not until graduate school in the mid-nineties that I was formally socialized to Left politics by Marxist intellectuals and through global justice movement organizing. As we disrupted meetings of the International Monetary Fund and World Trade Organization, Bernie was actively campaigning against Wall Street deregulation and corporate-friendly trade deals like the North American Free Trade Agreement (NAFTA) from inside the House of Representatives.

Antiwar activism dominated progressives' agenda in the early part of the millennium, but the 2007 financial crisis helped bring the US Left (and the Right, in the form of the Tea Party) back to confronting financial and corporate elites and their expanding influence over US elections. The constituency for Bernie's rails against Wall Street and big money in politics was broadening thanks to Occupy Wall Street, especially after he filed a constitutional amendment to overturn *Citizens United* and filibustered on the Senate floor for nine hours after Obama cut a deal with the GOP to extend the Bush tax cuts.

I was writing about the Occupy Wall Street protests at the time and wanted to understand how the elite political institutions that the movement was contesting functioned at the highest levels—so I embarked on a remake of C. Wright Mills's classic text, *The Power Elite*. A year working in Congress, I reasoned, could offer the kind of ethnographic perspective that most studies of power elites severely lacked.

In one of those rare instances in which the loose ends of a previous life tie up seamlessly into the present, I applied for, and was awarded, a congressional fellowship co-sponsored by the American Sociological Association and the American Association for the Advancement of Science (AAAS). I had worked as an administrative assistant for that very same AAAS program upon graduating from college exactly two decades earlier. It was the first time in the program's fifty-year history that an entry-level staffer returned as a postdoctoral awardee.

During our intensive two-week orientation, congressional fellows were treated to a crash course on federal budgeting, House and Senate floor procedure, and the looming sequestration and debt ceiling. Benghazi was lighting up around that time; so too were debates regarding the Senate's sixty-vote majority rule. We were warned that on the Hill, politics often trumps scientific fact and that the number of bills passed in the 112th Congress totaled less than half of those passed over the previous four years. Congress had descended into severe partisan gridlock, and the country was about to plunge over a "fiscal cliff."

At the close of the fortnight, we were invited to a "mixer" at the US Capitol to meet informally with prospective offices. We were free labor, but the placement process was still competitive. Previous fellows placed in Bernie's office warned me that it was no place for hotshots and that his leading political-economy staffer operated as a "lone wolf." Most fellows entered the program to secure postdoctoral employment in their expert fields, but I already had a job. For me, it was Bernie or bust.

At the mixer, I made a beeline for his chief of staff, Huck Gutman, a poetry professor from the University of Vermont. There, under the dome in the US Capitol,

Huck and I talked about climate change, the 1 percent, and Murray Bookchin, the famous Vermont anarchist. It was all good until the following day, when an email arrived from Huck confirming the worst: "Sorry, Heather, but we really just need an Environment person."

Other fellows were gaining on each other in second and third rounds of interviews, so I hit the pavement. I met with staffers (and a golden retriever) in Senator Al Franken's office, and with Congressman Ed Markey's chief of staff, who, I found out at the mixer, had authored an award-winning paper on the May 1968 protests in France. I also interviewed in Senator Chris Coons's office but likely overstepped with a mini-rant against policymakers' neutering of the Volcker Rule.

The situation felt rather desperate, until Huck rang. Within fifteen minutes, I was sitting next to Bernie, discussing my consulting work with trade unions like Service Employees International Union, trying hard not to look nervous. It was then that I got my first dose of the senator's particular charm: "Are you a good writer?" he asked. "Yes, I think so," I said sheepishly, "I got a piece published in the *Washington Post*." "Yeah," he said bluntly, "everyone thinks they're a good writer." Huck generously named other media outlets where I'd published, but Bernie cut to the chase: "Okay, okay. You're hired."

The next time I saw him was at Folsom Elementary in South Hero, a small town on an island in the middle of Lake Champlain. Driving past the picturesque apple orchards and boundless green pastures, it was clear why he'd traded in big city life for Vermont. On a rainy Sunday afternoon at the small town's elementary school, fifty or more gathered to watch him give a rousing forty-five-minute speech about how the big banks and Koch brothers were corrupting America. I saw him give another, more fiery one later that night in the northern part of the state, and again, a few weeks later, down in Putney. Each time he gave a speech, the crowds were so large that organizers had to close the doors on account of the fire code. He was far ahead in the polls but remained committed to hitting every county in the state.

That morning in South Hero, he grabbed a few folding chairs from a nearby stack and gave me my first set of marching orders: I was to compile an extensive research memo on universal health care, tuition-free college, public pensions, and other aspects of European democratic socialism. "And professor," he said wryly, "make it clear and to the point. This isn't academia. *Our classroom has 300 million people in it.*"

The night Bernie won his second term as a US senator, I was unpacking boxes in my new Washington, DC, apartment, gearing up to work for him. The work arrangement could not have been more different than what I enjoyed as a professor: a private office, summers off, and professional autonomy. My Senate office without walls was less than five feet from the round table where most constituent meetings took place—a front-row seat to impromptu political debates, office drama, and the daily parade of constituents and staffers from other offices. Not once did I see a corporate lobbyist or big leaguer from the NGO class. What I did see was a lot of public school kids and teachers, as well as environmentalists, veterans, and trade unionists. His staff dedicated themselves to their issue areas and, like academics, relished it when their deep digs had tangible impact. Those in his inner circle perpetually bent over backwards to respond to an unforgiving news cycle. Everyone wanted to whisper in the senator's ear.

Much of the policy basis and political agenda that fueled Bernie's presidential campaign can be traced to his nearly three decades in the House and the Senate. Even as a new-comer, I had little trouble predicting his issue positions because of the reliability and simplicity of his framework: If it was good for working-class people and the poor, he was for it, and if it was bad for them, he was opposed.

The European socialism project that he proposed to me back at Folsom Elementary involved preparing background on social welfare systems in Europe, and Denmark in par-ticular, where safety nets are in place so that normal events in a person's life—like sickness, unemployment, childbirth, aging—are not economically or socially ruinous. The goal of my assignment was to delineate the nuts and bolts of social wage policy and to help make Bernie's point that practices deemed inefficient and untenable in the United States are not as technically or politically controversial elsewhere.

Little did I know that his campaign would elevate this line of political thinking to the heights of US political discourse and that his lone voice promoting social democratic policies in the Senate would resonate so widely among the Amer-ican people. In hindsight, though, the signs of "political revolution" were always there. Early that fellowship year,

Huck called me into Bernie's office to sit in on a meeting with Karen Nussbaum, the executive director of Working America. He was inquiring about Working America's reach in southern red states and wanted to find ways to expand progressive networks in the region. Several months later, he made a "southern swing" to South Carolina, Georgia, Mississippi, and Alabama, visiting community health centers, union halls, and progressive groups' gatherings.

Four years after that meeting with Nussbaum, on the campaign trail in 2016, I met doctoral students from the University of South Carolina who recalled that southern swing. They appreciated Bernie's visit, they said, because the Democratic Party had totally abandoned its progressive base there.

After my fellowship year in Bernie's office, my husband and I sold our house in New Hampshire and moved to Ferrisburgh, Vermont. I resumed teaching at Fordham but stayed connected to Bernie's office through friendships with his staff. During that period, I published about a dozen opinion pieces on his policies, including a June 2014 essay in the *Washington Post* on whether he should run for president. Bernie had been using the term "political revolution," but pundits still treated him as a protest candidate. I argued that he should throw his hat into the ring because while Hillary's appeal to identity politics would rally corporate feminists, it would do little to unite and empower America's disenfranchised or move the dial on social inequality.

I also predicted in the essay that social class was going to be the major axis on which the new US politics would emerge—but questioned whether that dynamic would "arouse a progressive turn or degenerate into the paranoid hooliganism of some on the radical right." In the end, I asserted that Bernie's

> "political revolution" may seem overly ambitious given how corrupt and partisan our political system has become, but it's no more ambitious than convincing poor and middle-class people that Sheldon Adelson and Goldman Sachs share their interests—or that Hillary Clinton and Chris Christie do, either.[7]

Class *did* end up as the fundamental organizing principle of US politics in 2016. And it aroused both a progressive turn in the person of Bernie Sanders and a degenerate right-wing hooliganism in the person of Donald Trump. What I did not see coming in June 2014, however, was how establishment Democrats would use gender and racial inequality to undermine progressive alternatives—and just how badly that strategy would backfire. There are myriad reasons for the outcome of 2016. But it's undeniable that the Clinton campaign's profound ignorance of the needs of poor and working-class Americans provided easy fodder for Trump and his appeals to "the silent majority"—those talked down to by "the lying liberal media" and left out of the Democrats' New Economy.

This book begins the story of Bernie's remarkable presidential campaign with a brief sojourn through Democratic Party politics from the seventies onward. It discusses Bernie's thorny relationship to the political establishment over the years and his uneasy decision to run as a Democrat, despite being the longest serving Independent in congressional history.

Subsequent chapters identify some of the major contradictions in Democratic Party politics that Bernie's campaign brought to light and that enabled Trump's political ascendancy. Those chapters follow the trajectory of Bernie's campaign—its dramatic success and ultimate roadblocks—and the dizzying events leading up to and following the general election. The book ends with a discussion of where we go from here and how Bernie's political agenda, and the political movements that coalesced around it, can help Americans pick up the pieces and move forward.

1
Crashing the Party

"Every man a King," he recalled, cutting into one of the meatballs on his plate. "*That* was his big slogan. That, and 'Share the Wealth.'" It was the same spaghetti and meatballs he'd ordered the last time we met for dinner, and the time before that. "He built hundreds of bridges and roadways throughout the state ..."

I had just returned from New Orleans and was recounting a conversation I'd had with a cab driver down there about former Louisiana governor Edwin Edwards. Bernie's segue to Huey Long was almost immediate: "Long ran on redistributing wealth and helping the poor. He was probably the most famous populist in American history"—he moved his arms up and down, much like Long—"known for his firebrand speeches, yuge crowds ..."

As his fork rejoined the heap of pasta before him, the senator rattled off a series of reforms: Social Security, universal health care, free textbooks and higher education, minimum wage increases and a basic income guarantee, public works, capping wealth and taxing it—all of which sounded like his own platform. He didn't romanticize The Kingfish—his hideous racism, abuses of power, flamboyance that would make even Donald Trump blush. But Long's championing of the powerless against corporate giants like JP Morgan and Standard Oil clearly resonated with him. It resonated with me, too.

One of the first things I'd read about Bernie while preparing to work in his office was that he carried Eugene Debs's keychain in his pocket. I felt a kind of kinship with him, because I too possessed a similar prized relic: an original Socialist Party charter certificate with Debs's name handwritten in quivering block letters. Huey Long was a hot mess. But Debs was the antithesis of the adage that a great man cannot be a good man. A fierce crusader against worker exploitation and imperialist war, he despised capitalism, "a monstrous system," as he called it, and fought the power on the heels of the Gilded Age, building worker organizations and the party itself. The same year that John D. Rockefeller became America's first billionaire, Debs ran for a fourth time as the Socialist Party's presidential candidate, capturing 6 percent of the vote, as some 1,200 other Socialists won seats in local and state government.

During the 2016 primary, Bernie's political identity and use of the term "democratic socialist" drew multiple story lines. Some leftists complained that he wasn't "really a socialist," and they insulted his supporters by alleging that he was sheep-dogging them. Establishment liberals and conservatives openly red-baited him, while the

National Review and other far-right news sources alluded to Stalin, the Gulag, and even the Yugo. More nuanced assessments referenced anti-austerity, resistance to neo-liberalism, and a clarion call for a new Keynesianism. The latter included Thomas Piketty's essay in the *Guardian*, where he credited Bernie with having revived the United States' "tradition of egalitarianism," against the status quo agenda of Hillary Clinton, "just another heiress of the Reagan-Clinton-Obama political regime."[1]

Critiques of Bernie's authenticity as a socialist tended to operate at the periphery of discourses regarding the significance of his challenge to the prevailing political-economic order. Bernie used the slogan "political revolution" to signify the extent to which his program veered from the establishment status quo, but leftists were understandably opposed to his use of the word "revolution" in that context, as his campaign was not calling for a radical social and political restructuring of power and authority in the United States, like modern revolutionary movements had in Cuba, Bolivia, and elsewhere. Bernie did not associate himself with anticapitalist politics or seek to nationalize major industries (though he has in the past). Rather, he advocated for increasing government regulation and corporate taxation and removing elements of the social system, like health care and higher education, from the market economy. He also promoted policies to revive public investment and social safety nets, in housing, poverty relief, and jobs and income policy—much like the industrial Keynesianism of the postwar era, yet without the behemoth militarism and uneven "compromises" between capital and labor. His goal was to help improve the lives of working-class people and expose how exploitation by the rich and powerful was robbing them of the opportunity to live the good life.

Early in the primary campaign, the distinguished historian Eric Foner penned an open letter to Bernie in the *Nation*, lauding him for his emphasis on "the active involvement of the federal government" over market-driven policies, and beckoning him to replace his references to European social welfare with examples from "the rich heritage of American radicalism"—for example, FDR's New Deal and Second Bill of Rights and A. Philip Randolph's "A Freedom Budget for All Americans."[2] A few weeks later, as if on cue, Bernie delivered his celebrated "democratic socialism" speech at Georgetown University with only brief mention of European systems and instead invoking FDR's New Deal and Johnson's Great Society: "Roosevelt implemented a series of programs that put millions of people back to work, took them out of poverty and restored their faith in government," he said. "This country has socialism for the rich and rugged individualism for the poor."[3]

In his letter, Foner also drew parallels between Bernie's politics and the morality underlying Debs's socialism— their ability to conjure collective outrage over the just plain wrongness of social inequality in the United States and their conviction that everyday people could make profound social change through the exercise of political power: "It was Debs's moral fervor as much as his specific program that made him beloved by millions of Americans."[4] Debs's socialism was less about setting "a blueprint for a future society," Foner explained, than about political leaders' moral obligation "to rein in the excesses of capitalism ... to empower ordinary people in a political system verging on plutocracy, and to develop policies that make opportunity real for the millions of Americans for whom it is not." His point was not to downplay Debs's anticapitalism but to highlight the mass emotional resonance of his indignation over social injustice and to show how Bernie was uniquely taking up that mantle.

Prominent campaign surrogate Cornel West also defined Bernie's program in moral terms, calling it "neopopulist" —which he described as the "principled use of the government to come to the rescue of working and poor people crushed by Wall Street greed and upper middle-class indifference to the disappearing opportunities of vulnerable fellow citizens."[5]

Indeed, Bernie has been railing against social inequality and the undue power of the wealthy for many decades. In the mid-seventies, he called for the Rockefeller family fortune to be broken up and used to pay for government programs for the poor and elderly. His denunciations against "Wall Street greed" throughout the eighties and nineties included an impassioned floor speech against Reagan's bailout of miscreant Savings and Loans in 1991—in addition to frequent grillings of pharmaceutical giants and their bipartisan enablers in Congress.

Into the new millennium, Bernie famously chastised Alan Greenspan at a 2003 House Committee on Financial Services hearing, where he told the Fed chairman, right to his face, that he was "way out of touch with the needs of middle-class and working families of our country" and was using his position "to represent the wealthy and large corporations."[6]

Since the *Citizens United* decision in 2010, he's turned a laserlike focus on "extremist," "right-wing billionaires" like the Koch brothers and Sheldon Adelson as part of an ongoing, high-profile counteroffensive against the far Right's war of ideas and the outsized influence of wealthy elites in US politics.[7]

The perplexity of the 2016 presidential race was not whether Bernie was *really* a socialist, or Trump *really* a racist, but that large portions of the electorate embraced them both despite these taboo identities. Pundits marveled at polls conducted by the *New York Times* and other news outlets that suggested a majority of Democrats, even Clinton supporters, viewed socialism in a positive light. It's unclear what that meant, however, given the historical ambiguity of the concept. Most Americans view socialism negatively and associate it with authoritarian states, which severely limits the ability of US politicians to push any kind of anticapitalist, or even mildly social democratic, agenda through the institutions of government. Bernie's association with socialism may have meant something to the Left, and to the Right, but for the masses of people with less honed political identities, it was largely beside the point.

What did matter, crucially, were the numerous polls that indicated, during and after the election, that Americans support a more even distribution of income and wealth, the expansion of programs like Social Security and Medicare, increasing the minimum wage, and getting big money out of politics. Democrats paid lip service to these issues and "rebuilding the middle class," but their candidate proceeded with a means-tested and overly bureaucratized policy platform that bored voters and looked like more of the same. Hillary Clinton's historically low popularity and image as a corrupt "establishment" politician can be attributed in part to that contradiction. But it was her frequent flip-flops on trade, her association with husband Bill's draconian crime and welfare reform policies, and the couple's conspicuous ties to Silicon Valley and Wall Street that did her and her party in.

Democrats and the Age of Inequality

Distinguished historian Judith Stein chronicled the emergence of the "Age of Inequality" in her aptly titled book on the seventies, *Pivotal Decade*.[8] In the decades leading up to that fundamental shift, Cold War militarism and pro-growth ideology brought compromise between an emboldened working class with post-Depression desires for prosperity, and tightly organized, class-conscious state and business elites. Those forces converged in the postwar years to defeat social democratic policies and state planning. Instead of universal health care, free college, and full employment, a commercial, market-based form of Keynesianism prevailed, offering tax breaks, wage increases, and other economic incentives. For workers, the carrot of consumption was exchanged for a kind of productivity that outpaced wage increases and other demands.[9]

Bernie was in his early adulthood when the working-class rebellions of the late sixties and early seventies—from wildcat strikes to urban riots—cut into the profit margins of an ascendant corporate America—as did environmental, consumer protection, and anticolonial and antiwar movements and sharp increases in food and oil prices. Free market ideologues like the Chicago School's Milton Friedman, and far-right anti-statists like Fred Koch and the John Birch Society, tried to wage a class war to recover declining profits, using widely cherished concepts like liberty, freedom, and choice. Working to discredit government regulation, progressive taxation, and public institutions, they built think tanks, academic institutes, and their own media outlets. Their views were considered fringe by most mainstream conservatives until the late 1970s, when a fresh generation—led by right-wing billionaires like Charles and David Koch, Richard Mellon Scaife, and John M. Olin— used their fortunes to build an incredible propaganda machine and infiltrate the Republican Party.

Gordon Lafer documented how the National Association of Manufacturers, the US Chamber of Commerce, and Business Roundtable did their part by opposing consumer protection and lobbying to defang the Humphrey-Hawkins bill, which would have instituted a legal right to a job, with the federal government as employer of last resort. Their assistance in defeating labor law reform—which would have made it easier for workers to form unions—"represented the biggest mobilization of corporate pressure to date," according to Lafer.[10]

Keynesianism's persistent struggle to balance employment with rising inflation offered a viable rationale for turning to supply-side solutions. Though the crisis of profitability in the 1970s was *the* fundamental crisis, the confluence of unemployment and runaway inflation ("stagflation") bolstered arguments that Keynesianism was imploding and that "big government" was inherently flawed. Supply-side advocates also used stagflation to legitimize the repressive Volcker shock, which ushered grueling levels of unemployment and cuts in public spending. The same kind of shock therapy was used as "an experiment" on the Chilean people in 1973 under Kissinger and Nixon and on New Yorkers in 1976 during the city's fiscal crisis. In both cases, the retrenchments and privatizations were driven by ultrawealthy financiers, many of them acolytes of Milton Friedman, the godfather of neoliberalism.

The neoliberal austerity politics of the 1970s can be blamed on conservatives and Republican leadership, but Jimmy Carter, a Democrat, also played a vital role. As Georgia's governor, he dedicated himself to ending "government waste" and inefficiency and, as president, mixed that program with deregulation in key industries, like transportation and finance. In a televised speech on October 24, 1978, Carter announced: "We are going to hold down government spending, reduce the budget deficit, and eliminate government waste. We will slash Federal hiring and cut the Federal work force. We will eliminate needless regulations."[11] That same day he signed into law the Airline Deregulation Act. By removing price controls, the act intensified mergers and labor market competition and thus reduced airline workers' benefits and drove down their wages.[12] Carter also acquiesced to corporate tax breaks and removed Regulation Q interest rates ceilings, which opened countless opportunities for financial exploitation, from sub-prime mortgage lending to payday loans that dispossess vulnerable people of their meager incomes.[13]

It wasn't until Reagan's presidency that the neoliberal agenda was brought to flower, however, with massive tax cuts for the wealthy and corporate welfare. Corporations were incentivized to expand employment; and the strong dollar during Reagan's first term hurt exports and made it cheaper for companies to invest in properties overseas. They used the money to relocate production offshore and to right-to-work states with the result that workers were essentially subsidizing the outsourcing of their own jobs. Then US taxpayers were told that in order to hold down the deficit, they had to accept cuts in public programs.

Massive state divestment in essential social services and institutions ensued—in fields like education, health care, housing, employment, wages, poverty relief, and pensions —as did legislative shifts in tax, monetary, and employment policy away from full employment and living wages and toward upward wealth redistribution and fiscal austerity. Privatization schemes tendered as "economic development" and the liberalization of financial institutions precipitated major international economic crises, in 1982 and 1987, and a massive dispossession of foreign resources by way of neocolonial structural adjustment. The profitability crisis for America's ruling class was resolved by the 1 percent of wealth-holders nearly doubling their share of the nation's wealth, one of the fastest escalations of upward wealth transfer in modern US history.[14]

Mark Dudzic and Adolph Reed, Jr., define *neoliberalism*

as a form of "capitalism that has effectively eliminated working-class opposition."[15] That includes, specifically, the decline of trade unions and worker power since the 1970s (and earlier), and the tendency of today's labor institutions to operate as appendages of the political establishment. Such tendencies are in part due to labor's successive legislative defeats on full employment, collective bargaining rights, wage protections, and so on, as well as what former Communications Workers of America president Larry Cohen described as "labor leaders regularly mingl[ing] with Democratic Party leaders and big-money party funders," which, for public sector workers, is often a necessary part of budget battles and protecting their members' jobs.[16]

As Dudzic and Reed, Jr., point out, these trends are an important element in, if not a driver of, the more general erosion of collective political life on which neoliberal capitalism feeds. Reagan and his British counterpart, Margaret Thatcher, paved the way for these ideological trends, mixing Cold War anticommunism with the stagflation-driven strife of the Carter years and with the Winter of Discontent in the United Kingdom. They positioned union bureaucracy and government regulation as agents of unfreedom and waste and demonized "big government" with appeals to personal freedom and responsibility. In the Reagan–Thatcher worldview, society was just a sum of self-interested individuals, and class inequality a fact of human nature.[17]

Regarding the Democratic Party's "fiscal responsibility" strategy in the 1984 race against Reagan, Peter T. Kilborn wrote in the *New York Times*, "Close your eyes, listen to what they're saying and you'd think it was the G.O.P."[18] In all fairness, Democratic nominee Walter Mondale's deficit reduction platform was actually focused on increasing taxes, reducing defense spending, and containing health care costs, rather than cutting social programs as Reagan had.[19] But still, Kilborn was not wrong. With Republicans having quadrupled the national debt by 1992, Democratic presidential candidate Senator Paul Tsongas brought to the national stage his conservative manifesto, *A Call to Economic Arms*, which painted a doomsday picture of "crushing and unsustainable debt" that, he argued, necessitated entitlement reform and a cut in the capital gains tax to encourage long-term investment.[20]

In the crosshairs was Social Security, which Reagan, along with Alan Greenspan, had already tried, and failed, to privatize. After resigning from the primary, Tsongas joined now billionaire Pete Peterson under the Durst debt clock to co-found a bipartisan "entitlement reform" group called the Concord Coalition. A notorious deficit hawk, Peterson had long been trying to privatize Social Security, Medicare, and Medicaid, dating at least back when he was chairman of Lehman Brothers in the mid-1970s.

Also in the race in 1992 was billionaire Ross Perot, who advocated means-testing programs like Social Security and Medicare and claimed that he could save $20 billion by cutting benefits. Bill Clinton called Perot's plan "a full-scale assault on the Social Security system, undermining the universality of the program."[21] But Clinton too had run on a program of "leaner, not meaner government" and "no more something for nothing." His acceptance speech for the Democratic Party nomination telegraphed how his "new covenant" would cut entitlements, facilitate school choice, and promote "a new approach to government ... that understands that jobs must come from growth in a vibrant and vital system of free enterprise."[22]

President Clinton's 1993 budget plan came under fire from Nebraska Democratic senator Bob Kerrey for not being tough enough on the middle class. To secure Kerrey's vote, Clinton agreed to form the Bipartisan Commission on Entitlement and Tax Reform to study entitlements. He appointed Peterson to the group and recommended that the Concord Coalition team up with the American Association of Retired Persons (AARP) to sponsor town hall meetings on entitlement reform around the country. (The AARP loathed Peterson so much they requested a proxy.)[23]

Peterson was one of just four or five members of the commission who supported Kerrey's proposed cuts and privatization schemes.[24] They failed to reach consensus, but conservative economist Martin Feldstein still applauded Clinton's efforts:

> The Clinton speeches and the official national education campaign that he launched moved the discussion of investment-based Social Security reform away from an ideological debate about the merits of government versus private systems to the more technical issues of how to design a mixed system that includes both pay-as-you go benefits and investment-based defined contribution annuities.[25]

It was an early harbinger of the Clintons' signature methodology of using technocratic means to remove social democratic alternatives from America's political horizon, while financializing vital public services and institutions.

The Party of Clinton

In August 1996, the *Nation*'s Katha Pollitt wrote a scathing critique of Bill Clinton's welfare reform agenda titled "The Strange Death of Liberal America."[26] She opened the piece with a lament over Linda Chavez-Thompson's performance at the 1996 Democratic Party Convention, where the AFL-CIO's first female and minority vice president gave "a resounding thumbs up" to the Democratic Party's platform, which included Republican-authored language on welfare reform.[27] For Pollitt, the Democrats' embrace of GOP-inspired welfare ideology, and the lack of grassroots resistance to it by trade union leaders like Chavez-Thompson, was officially signaling the end of American New Deal liberalism. She was right: When Margaret Thatcher was asked in 2002 about her greatest achievement as prime minister, she replied, "Tony Blair and New Labour. We forced our opponents to change their minds."[28]

The same could be said of Reagan's achievement in Bill Clinton and the New Democrats. The Democratic Leadership Council (DLC) was founded during Reagan's presidency in 1985, after three major electoral losses— Jimmy Carter, Walter Mondale, and Michael Dukakis. It wanted to shift the party toward "the center" where it believed national elections were won. Reverend Jesse Jackson's quip that the DLC stood for "Democrats for the Leisure Class" correctly identified the New Democrats' underlying class program, which was manifest in Clinton's agenda to foster "growth" and "opportunity" by way of small government and "personal responsibility."

The hundreds of thousands of manufacturing jobs that were lost during Reagan's presidency spurred a crack epidemic in formerly working-class inner-city neighborhoods, and crime rates soared. The 1994 midterm elections—the "Gingrich Revolution"—shifted the political dynamic rightward, and according to polls, a majority of Americans favored welfare reform. Clinton vetoed a few GOP versions of welfare reform bills but followed through on his campaign promise "to end welfare as we know it."

Temporary Assistance for Needy Families (TANF) rendered welfare programs for poor families temporary and precarious. It replaced the federal safety net with a block grant to the states, added work requirements, imposed a five-year lifetime limit on assistance, and barred undocumented immigrants from licensed professions. Workfare required mothers to work for their benefits and, without daycare provisions, put many children at risk. The number of very poor Americans surviving on incomes of $2/day doubled to 1.5 million over the decade and a half that followed. During the Great Recession of 2007, when TANF was most needed, several states cut their programs to close budget shortfalls.[29]

Bill Clinton accused conservatives of using race to divide the nation, but he adopted their disciplinary approach to poverty and crime, using similarly racist ideology to exploit cultural anxieties. He echoed Reagan's invectives against "welfare queens" and being "tough on crime"; and years later, as first lady, Hillary called young black teens "super-predators" and said they needed to be "brought to heel." Instead of using government programs to stimulate youth employment and stem the downward spiral of poverty and incarceration, the Clintons and their party spoke of personal responsibility and free markets as keys to social mobility.[30]

Bill Clinton oversaw the largest prison inmate increase of any US president. White Americans saw historic reductions in rates of unemployment, but for black men in their twenties without a college degree, unemployment rose to its highest levels—42 percent in 2001, when Clinton left office—which was largely due to skyrocketing incarceration rates. The Clinton administration eliminated federal higher education grants for prisoners, denied financial aid to students with drug convictions, and supported a lifetime ban on food stamps for those convicted of a felony drug offense. It also tried to deny public housing and shelter to any person with a criminal history, including minor offenses. Billions were transferred from public housing and child welfare budgets to fund the newly emerging carceral state. Public housing funding was cut 61 percent, while funding for corrections was boosted by 171 percent.[31]

In addition to mortally wounding America's social welfare system and causing the country's incarceration rate to soar (making it the highest in the world), President Clinton advocated free trade and the deregulation of global financial markets—powered by new computing and communications technologies that enlarged trading capacities and innovations and transformed financial instruments like derivatives into tradable commodities. The new wave of financial instruments was supposed to hedge against the perils of high-risk lending while securing the housing market and other essential institutions from the vicissitudes of globalization. But it also multiplied opportunities for high-risk, speculation-driven profit-making that raised stock prices to the heavens, making many of the billionaires who now top the *Forbes* list.[32]

Tech and finance moguls did phenomenally well, but the lion's share of those profits were enjoyed by very few. Between 1989 and 1997, 86 percent of stock market gains went to the top 10 percent of households, and 42 percent went to the top 1 percent of them. For most Americans, however, debt outgrew assets, and the net worth of median US households declined from the eighties to the mid-nineties (from $51,640 to $49,900). Low-income and poor families registered negative net worth.

After two terms of George W. Bush—that is, eight years of enormous tax cuts for the rich, draconian education reform (No Child Left Behind), the horrific Iraq and Afghanistan wars, Hurricane Katrina, and an epic, manmade financial crisis—Barack Obama became president on a platform to end war, promote civil and human rights, make government more transparent, stimulate the economy, and re-regulate Wall Street. Like most major crises, the financial meltdown in 2007 offered the possibility of a sea change. But Obama largely stayed the course, doubling down on Bush's drone strikes, spying on US citizens,[33] and using conservatives' "tough love" approach to the poor. With references to "Cousin Pookie" and feeding one's children "cold Popeye's for breakfast," Obama revealed a sordid view of poor black men as shiftless and lazy, squandering their hard-won right to vote, in distinction to industrious, upper-class black men like him, graced with a higher sense of purpose.[34]

One of Obama's first major accomplishments as president was a massive Wall Street bailout that involved a series of secret loans and side bailouts, without relief for the masses of people enduring epidemic foreclosure, job loss, and agonizing recession. The lack of recovery assistance on Main Street helped provoke a Great Recession that not only tanked Obama's popularity but also fanned the flames of a coming right-wing offensive. The Tea Party was just one expression of the vastly enlarged network of social and corporate media, think tanks, and academic institutes that gathered force in the wake of the recession. The Koch brothers' fledging political network that had been operating at the fringes expanded exponentially with a near trillion dollar war chest by 2016.[35]

The Right laughably, but effectively, deemed Obama a "socialist," but he himself scoffed at the label and described his presidency as "entirely consistent with free-market principles."[36] It was: He cut public sector investment and failed to impose a tax on the wealthy as he had promised. In collaboration with Education Secretary Arne Duncan, a Teach for America champion, he facilitated K through 12 privatization by touting charter schools and instituting Darwinian education reform, tellingly named "Race to the Top." He positioned the Trans-Pacific Partnership as a signature item on his agenda—a massive, corporate-driven free trade deal, brokered in secret, that was estimated to cost US jobs, reduce wages, and further deregulate critical industries.[37]

Obama *did* help reduce unemployment and increase real median income, though slightly, and he saved countless auto workers' jobs. He spoke out against *Citizens United* and, under Obamacare, expanded health insurance coverage to record numbers of Americans, though he did so by taking single-payer health care off the table.[38] But Democrats controlled the White House for sixteen of the twenty-four years before Trump's election and, for four of them, both chambers of Congress. All that time, the dial on wealth inequality continued to tick upward, and labor unions weakened, as corporate power further consolidated. From the perspective of income and wealth inequality, the New Democrats' class program was hardly discernible from that of the GOP. In both cases, the American State was openly operating as the executive of the ruling class, and it was doing so with little opposition.

Bernie and the Democratic Party

Bernie's entry into the 2016 primary offered an escape hatch from the New Democrats' ruling class agenda with a platform to redistribute the country's wealth more evenly, re-regulate financial institutions, and empower working people through full employment—in addition to confronting the climate crisis, mass incarceration, and permanent war. He was uniquely situated to run such a campaign within the context of the Democratic Party primary, having caucused with the Democrats for many years without pledging his political allegiance to them.

Bernie has marked his political identity over the years by

taking on both parties. In the mid-eighties, he called them "cowardly" and remarked incisively that "the main difference between the Democrats and the Republicans in this city [Burlington, Vermont] is that the Democrats are in insurance and the Republicans are in banking."[39] In a *New York Times* op-ed in 1989, he caricatured the two major parties as "Tweedledee" and "Tweedledum," and that same year said they constituted "one party—the party of the ruling class."[40] Even when supporting Walter Mondale's candidacy and, later, Jesse Jackson's, Bernie made his political loyalties abundantly clear: "I am not a Democrat, period."[41]

Bernie's antagonism to Democrats was manifest not just in rhetoric but also in legislative substance. During his service in the House of Representatives from 1991 to 2007, and later since becoming a US senator, he took principled stances against Presidents Clinton and Obama's signature policies—from "welfare reform" to free trade agreements (FTAs) to Wall Street deregulation. As chairman of the Congressional Progressive Caucus in the mid-nineties, he spoke out against conservative propaganda demonizing the poor and instead demonized politicians willing to cut school lunch programs to fund tax cuts for the rich. He was vehement in his opposition to Bill Clinton's North American Free Trade Agreement (NAFTA) on behalf of workers and the environment and equally vocal against subsequent FTAs, which Hillary and Obama continued to promote, despite massive FTA-induced job losses.

Bernie also went after New Democrats' efforts to liberalize the financial sector. In the wake of the 1929 stock market crash, FDR signed the Glass-Steagall Act to prevent massive bank failure and protect consumers' deposits and taxpayer dollars by creating a firewall between commercial and investment banks. Banks like Walter Wriston's Citicorp had been lobbying Congress to ease Glass-Steagall restrictions since the 1960s, as money markets and other financial instruments were blurring the lines between deposits and securities. Wriston and other big bankers wanted to operate across state lines and form "one-stop shopping" conglomerates.

President Carter began the process of liberalizing finance by phasing out interest rate ceilings and allowing commercial banks and Savings and Loans to compete with money markets. Savings and Loans were meant to serve the expanding housing market as a kind of anti-redlining public service, but with shifts in the regulatory climate under Reagan and intensified speculation, it was fast becoming a shady business.[42] When thousands of thrifts failed and threatened the stability of the financial system, US taxpayers paid over $124 billion in bailout monies—a harbinger of the subprime mortgage crisis in 2007.[43]

The Clinton administration carried the torch of financial liberalization by working closely with Republicans and Wall Street to repeal Glass-Steagall and by brazenly preventing governmental efforts to regulate derivatives and other high-risk vehicles. Bernie warned that further liberalization would result in megamergers, exorbitant consumer fees, and serious exposure to risk. But even after the 2007 financial crisis, proposed rules to resurrect the firewall between commercial and investment banks were defanged by a Wall Street–friendly Obama administration. Today, the country's largest financial institutions control tens of trillions in assets and have become even more opaque in their operations—and increasingly "too big to fail."[44]

During the signing of the Troubled Asset Relief Program (TARP)—also known as the Wall Street bailout—President Obama trumpeted: "Because of this law, the American people will never again be asked to foot the bill for Wall Street's mistakes. There will be no more tax-funded bailouts, period."[45] But what amounted to tens of trillions in government outlays involved not just TARP, but a series of additional bailout programs,[46] tax deferrals, and secret loans, some of which only became public after Bernie amended Dodd-Frank to force a rare, one-shot audit of the Fed.[47]

That audit is how we learned that while governors nationwide were firing public school teachers, canceling school bus services, and cutting vital services like Meals on Wheels, the Fed provided $176 trillion in virtually zero interest loans and other assistance to nearly every major bank in the country, as well as foreign banks and some of the largest corporations in the world. Banks parked the money in interest-bearing accounts and used it to subsidize lucrative mergers; some of them took out low-interest federal loans to repay the more expensive ones from TARP.[48] All of this happened under the watch of Ben Bernanke, a Bush and Obama appointee.

In light of his objections to these and other aspects of the New Democrats' agenda, Bernie's decision of whether to run as a Democrat was not an easy one. Bernie holds the title of the longest sitting Independent member of Congress in US history, and he is proud of that accomplishment. Weighing on his decision was his desire to maintain that status, and (following Ralph Nader's controversial run in 2000) to avoid having a spoiler effect that would benefit the Right. There was also the pragmatic question of how to get on the ballot in fifty states. Any Democrat or Republican who wins their party's nomination is guaranteed a place on each state's ballot for the general election, but in many states, third parties must petition election officials. There are significant barriers to obtaining ballot status, including sabotage from the two major parties. Bernie could have spent the entire campaign season mired in that struggle and may never have broken through the way he did.

In the lead-up to his announcement, Bernie toured the country: from New Hampshire to Illinois and Iowa, to Texas and the South, and out west to California. He solicited the opinions of various trade unions and progressive groups, including the Progressive Democrats of America, MoveOn.org, Democracy for America, and Ready for Warren, the well-funded and well-publicized effort to draft Senator Elizabeth Warren to run for president. Progressive Democrats were wary of a Clinton coronation, not just because of her conservative politics and Wall Street ties, but because it was not readily apparent that she could win. The party's steep electoral losses in 2014, when the Democrats lost control of the Senate for the first time since 2006, suggested that many Americans had had enough of the Clinton model. These and other groups wanted to see a competitive primary race, and they were mobilizing grassroots support for a progressive policy agenda.

Leadership within the party and the Democratic National Committee (DNC) was openly hostile to Bernie's entry into the race. DNC vice chair Donna Brazile tweeted on March 14, 2016, that it was "extremely disgraceful" for him to run as a Democrat, and Brad Woodhouse, a former DNC communications director, tweeted a day later that Bernie was "a political calculating fraud."[49] During the primary, a DNC chairwoman Debbie Wasserman Shultz went so far as to improperly shut off his campaign's access to voter files on bogus allegations of data tampering.[50] According to WikiLeaks, she conspired to discredit him on the basis of his religious beliefs, while Donna Brazile helped fix a CNN presidential debate by leaking some of the questions to Hillary's campaign.[51] About a year after Trump's election, Brazile released a tell-all of the 2016 race in which she exposed how the Clinton campaign rescued the Obama-bankrupted DNC and controlled its financial resources throughout the primary, at the expense of local party affiliates and the Bernie campaign.[52]

Elected officials in the Democratic Party delivered particularly vitriolic blows. In the lead-up to the New York primary, the *New York Daily News* published a story with the headline "Bernie's Sandy Hook Shame," in which Connecticut governor Dannel Malloy and members of his state's congressional delegation criticized Bernie's voting record on gun control by essentially blaming him for the Sandy Hook tragedy.[53] Members of the Congressional Black Caucus and Hispanic Caucus tried to defame him on matters of race and ethnicity, while Senator Claire McCaskill took to open red-baiting: "I think the media is giving Bernie a pass right now. I very rarely read in any coverage of Bernie that he is a Socialist," she said. "I think he would like to see Medicare for all." When his popularity soared, she instead jabbed at his age: "I love him! I mean he's a great old guy."[54]

Bernie's decision to run was also shaped by the question of how to raise enough money to be competitive in a presidential race and the related issue of how to be taken seriously by the corporate media. Hillary Clinton was arguably the most popular politician in the world, with a massive war chest and deep patronage networks. The organizational chart for her campaign resembled that of a major corporation. Bernie started off doing as many TV, radio, and print interviews as possible with local and national media, and he tested the waters with low-dollar fund-raising. When I asked a member of his inner circle about his decision to run without big money donors and Super PACs, he told me that it was really a no-brainer: Bernie has never run that kind of campaign, and he never will.

Money, media, and party status were all important factors, but his ultimate concern was that the campaign not devolve into a sideshow and risk discrediting progressive ideas more generally. His was an historic campaign on many levels, but one of its most important revelations was that every one of the economic and regulatory reforms that congressional Democrats rejected as untenable or "too left" were widely favored by the American public—from universal health care and education, to fair not "free" trade, to getting the rich to pay their fair share in taxes and not unduly influence elections. The other major, eye-opening revelation was that it is possible to run competitively for president of the United States on small donations averaging $27 and without Super PACs.

I visited Bernie's campaign office on Church Street a few times before he officially launched his campaign, when just a few staff members—Phil, Shannon, Hector—were plugging in the lamps and installing the computers. On May 26, 2015, that same office was teeming with staff members and volunteers. Media outlets that had written him off as a gadfly and protest candidate were starting to take serious notice. Bernie has long been critical of the corporate media for covering political drama in lieu of "the real issues," but his openness to reporters in the early days of the primary bore a stark contrast to Hillary's impudent roping them off.[55]

Bernie launched his presidential campaign on a perfect day by the shores of Lake Champlain on what turned out to be a deeply sentimental occasion. It was the same idyllic waterfront park that he helped build as Burlington's mayor decades earlier, and he was flanked by family and longtime friends, many of them stalwart progressives. The crowd count registered at 5,000 people, the largest political gathering in the modern history of the state. His speech echoed many others he'd given over the years, and yet on this occasion, it felt bigger, and more visionary: "Now is NOT the time for the same old same old establishment politics and stale Inside the Beltway ideas," he declared. "This campaign is not about Bernie Sanders. It is not about Hillary Clinton. It is not about Jeb Bush or anyone else. This campaign is about the needs of the American people, and the ideas and proposals that effectively address those needs."[56]

He went on to identify wealth and income inequality as "the great moral issue of our time" and talked about the disenfranchisement of ordinary Americans from the political process because of the power of big money in politics. "Combating this political alienation, this cynicism and this legitimate anger will not be easy; that's for sure. But that is exactly what, together, we have to do if we are going to turn this country around—and that is what this campaign is all about."[57]

2
The Campaign, Part 1:
Democratic Socialism

The Bernie Sanders campaign crashed the Democratic Party in 2016 by exposing the class interests its leadership represented and by expanding the horizon of political possibility in America. Newcomers to Bernie's political orbit remarked on how consistent he was in terms of his messaging and policy commitments, compared to most politicians who tend to blow with the political winds. That consistency derived from his commitment to working-class people of all races, genders, nationalities, sexualities, and creeds, which formed the basis of a coherent and principled political platform, distinct from the neoliberal political framework that had been guiding the Democratic Party's agenda for decades.

Bernie's "democratic socialism" includes a series of policy proposals aimed at eradicating poverty, rebuilding the working class, reinvesting in public institutions, and achieving a more equitable distribution of wealth in America. Specific aspects of his framework are discussed in the following pages, including efforts to curb the power of Wall Street and corporate America through financial, labor, and environmental regulation; opposition to job-killing free trade agreements; and tax policy that favors working-class people, not corporations and the rich. He has taken measures to address income and wealth inequality, including pushing for equal pay and minimum wage increases, empowering labor unions, and advocating for social wage policies—from universal health care and child care to free public college to land trusts, full employment, paid family leave, and so on. During the campaign, he offered a comprehensive plan for reforming US immigration policy, correctly positioned criminal justice as both a class and a civil rights issue, and called for an end to permanent war, in addition to his longtime fight against climate change and for sustainable energy.

Most of those policies and campaigns had been part of Bernie's political agenda for many years, but running for president offered a unique opportunity for his campaign to inject a comprehensive progressive platform into the national political discourse and expand Left and progressive coalitions around the country in support of it.

The Political Establishment

Campaign Finance

A necessary part of Bernie's agenda involved crashing the United States' corrupt campaign finance system. Ever since the Supreme Court's *Citizens United* decision in

2010, billions of dollars in "dark money" from the nation's wealthiest individuals have been flooding into US elections by way of Super PACs. Super PACs provide large corporations and the very rich with a legal means for funneling unlimited sums to electoral campaigns and exerting heavy influence over them, oftentimes more than candidates themselves, and more than traditional political parties.

Bernie proposed a constitutional amendment to overturn *Citizens United* and, over his nearly forty-year career, he has taken a principled stance against politicians using valuable legislating time to cozy up with donors. He himself has never taken corporate or Super PAC money; instead, he has opted to pass the hat around at local "town hall" meetings and solicit small donations through direct mail. He remained committed to small donor fund-raising for his presidential run in 2016, and over the course of the primary, participated in just nine or ten fund-raising events, most of them offering a sliding scale.

Establishment Democrats spoke out against *Citizens United*, but they continued to stage big money fund-raisers, rely on negative TV ads run by Super PACs, and court Wall Street and Silicon Valley elites behind closed doors. Hillary Clinton started the race with a gigantic war chest, and by the end of November 2016, she had raised a whopping $1.4 billion from her campaign and Super PACs, as well as party and joint fund-raising committees. That did not include the billions in donations to her family's namesake foundation, six-figure speaking fees, and monies derived from decades-old patronage networks that the *New York Review of Books* calculated as part of "the Clinton system."[1]

Most people thought Bernie's "purity" regarding campaign finance would discount him from presidential politics. But the opposite happened: He proved that it is possible to contend for high office in the United States without being corrupted by big money interests. Through online efforts, his campaign raised $228 million by way of 8.2 million individual contributions from 2.5 million people. The average donation was $27.[2]

Much of that inflow of small donations was enabled by social media. Even before 2016, Bernie had one of the largest digital followings of any US senator. Those numbers grew exponentially during his presidential run and proliferated his volunteer and donor database far beyond his and the Democrats' usual lists. The campaign's attention to new media widened his appeal among millennial voters, including the use of self-organized "house parties" that allowed him to reach millions of viewers at once using Livestream. He now has some 7.4 million Facebook friends and 5.6 million Twitter followers, exceeding mainstream media outlets like National Public Radio and C-SPAN.

Bernie's historic fund-raising accomplishments, his giant volunteer base, and his widespread appeal among progressive Democrats did not keep the party establishment from rallying around Clinton. She was the candidate who could "get things done," and, given the magnitude of her political organization, it was "her turn." Her massive organization involved high-end donors, Ivy League academics, trade union leaders, and heads of large-scale nonprofits—not to mention the thick underlayer of consultants, Super PAC managers, and political attack dogs who comprised her "external machine."

Most Democratic Party leaders at the national, state, and local levels had worked for the Clintons at some point or another. That extensive network brought her a 400 superdelegate lead out of the gate and nearly unanimous support in Congress. Just one (Senator Jeff Merkley) of forty-six Senate Democrats endorsed Bernie, and of the 187 Democratic congressmen and women, only nine openly supported him.[3] Establishment trade union leaders followed suit, despite sometimes vociferous opposition from their rank-and-file members.

Labor

A few months after the general election, the journal *New Labor Forum* published a 2016 postmortem with American Federation of Teachers (AFT) president Randi Weingarten and former Communications Workers of America president Larry Cohen on why US labor overwhelmingly supported Hillary Clinton. Both authors had been heavily involved in the primary race. Cohen served as a senior advisor to the Bernie campaign, and Weingarten, a longtime friend of Hillary's and board member of the pro-Clinton Super PAC Priorities USA Action, oversaw the AFT's endorsement of the former senator in the primaries.

In her essay, Weingarten, along with co-author Leo Casey, asserted that "most of the American labor movement endorsed Hillary for president … as the candidate that we believed had the best chance to win the 2016 election and enact a progressive policy agenda."[4] Cohen offered a very different view: "When they said Bernie can't win, what they really meant was that working-class people can't win."[5] His point was that the limits of political possibility set by establishment Democrats in the lead-up to 2016 largely denied the interests of poor and working-class people—and that many union leaders had come to accept those limits as given.

For Cohen, an endorsement for Clinton—whether based on risk calculation or actual political belief—signaled a rejection of progressive legislative priorities like single-payer health care, free public higher education, and a $15 minimum wage as constituting a politically tenable platform for presidential politics. An endorsement for Bernie, by contrast, affirmed a politics whose value was gauged not on whether the candidate was likely to win, but on how well it served the interests of regular people.

Labor unions should have been a natural constituency for Bernie. His agenda is decisively pro-worker; he has for many years opposed free trade deals that destroy US jobs and put downward pressure on wages. He believes in the power of collective bargaining, and his focus on economic inequality is unparalleled among today's politicians. For years, he's been introducing the Workplace Democracy Act, which aims to make it easier to join a union by allowing the National Labor Relations Board to certify a union if a simple majority of workers sign valid authorization cards.[6] He is an outspoken proponent of reinvesting in public institutions on which many working-class people rely. And over the years, he has walked countless picket lines in the fight for a living wage. The *Washington Post* remarked that while unions have suffered from low confidence among the

American public, Bernie was "bringing a more positive view of unions back into view."[7]

Because of the class interests that Bernie's campaign represented, his run in the Democratic primary brought to light important contradictions around labor's role in US politics. Republican-backed policies have long tended to favor big business, but for decades, establishment Democrats haven't been in workers' corner either. To be fair, political endorsements, depending on sector, can be complicated. For unions in government and education sectors, for example, elected officials have direct impact on budgets, pensions, health care, and other employment issues—as Cohen explained, "the distinction between lobbying and collective bargaining is very small."

But President Obama and the Democrats who supported him were to the right of Trump on the Trans-Pacific Partnership, the most important labor issue of 2016 and one in which the labor movement was unusually united in opposing. Hillary did not support a $15 minimum wage beyond her home state of New York until after the primary. And she continually argued that universal programs like single-payer and free public college were fiscally impossible, despite the US government's obscene spending on corporate welfare and defense and its central role in facilitating the country's extreme upward distribution of wealth.

Such trends are indicative of the very serious decline of America's middle class and the worker power that once undergirded it. Divestment from public institutions and successive defeats of working peoples' movements and organizations, alongside the automation, offshoring, and part-timing of tens of millions of jobs, has severely reduced trade union membership. The Department of Labor reported membership rates in the private sector at a mere 6.4 percent as of 2016 and just under 11 percent overall.[8] According to the US Bureau of Labor Statistics, the union membership rate in 2016 was half what it was in 1983.[9]

That weakness in numbers is exacerbated by attacks on collective bargaining itself, dating back to the postwar era when US corporations proliferated and anti-union campaigns were the norm. With groups like the Business Roundtable and the Heritage Foundation at their backs, the Right's ideological attacks have helped garner public mistrust of trade unions; in the present climate, most workers must navigate a minefield of threats and anti-union propaganda when engaging in organizing drives. Such threats have not been not idle: If an employee participates in a unionizing campaign, that person has a one in five chance of getting fired.

These and other dynamics necessarily shape internal questions regarding how union leaders relate to politicians and corporate management and how labor unions relate to grassroots movements. That such tensions rise to higher levels of public consciousness during presidential elections demonstrates how unions still hold some sway in US politics. But for 2016, the lion's share of labor leaders on the side of the Democratic Party did not operate as a progressive force, and in some instances, they actively tried to undermine pro-worker alternatives.

Bernie did get endorsements from national unions, including the Communications Workers of America

(200,000) and National Nurses United (NNU; 150,000), both of which played vital roles in the campaign, with Larry Cohen and NNU president RoseAnn DeMoro as close advisors. The Amalgamated Transit Union also supported him (250,000); so too did the American Postal Workers Union (200,000), the International Longshoremen's Association (35,000), and United Electrical, Radio and Machine Workers of America (20,000).

The NNU has been working with Bernie for many years to enact a single-payer health care system and on other progressive issues like the Robin Hood tax and opposition to free trade. During the campaign, it sponsored big red "Bernie Buses" to get out the vote around the country, and the National Nurses United for Patient Protection, an independent-expenditure political committee, spent over half a million on billboards and print and online ads.[10] Pundits cried hypocrisy given Bernie's opposition to Super PACs, but the expenditure was nowhere near the $12 million-plus spent by Ready for Hillary.[11]

DeMoro took up the campaign's mantle at the close of the primary by sponsoring a now annual event in Chicago called The Peoples' Summit, featuring activist workshops and popular speakers like Naomi Klein and Rosario Dawson and, in 2017, Bernie himself. Cohen now serves as board chairman of Our Revolution, a movement organization directly derived from the campaign.

In addition to national unions, labor union activists around the country organized "Labor for Bernie," with over 50,000 supporters. More than eighty locals endorsed him as well, some of them in opposition to their leaderships.[12]

They included several American Federation of Teachers, American Federation of State, County and Municipal Employees (AFSCME), and UNITE HERE locals, as well as the now famous United Steelworkers Local 1999, whose president, Chuck Jones, made headlines for calling out Donald Trump on his false claims regarding saving jobs at the Carrier plant in Indianapolis. During Local 1999's endorsement, Jones stated, "Bernie Sanders for decades has fought against the kinds of disastrous trade deals that are now allowing Carrier to ship over a thousand good-paying Indiana jobs to Mexico."[13]

The 5,000-member University of California branch of the AFT broke for Bernie, as did the South Carolina chapter of the AFL-CIO, which later had to roll back its endorsement when President Richard Trumka reprimanded them. The AFL-CIO needed a two-thirds majority of its executive council in order to issue an endorsement. But Trumka didn't have the votes, so he decided to withhold the endorsement until after the primary, which was a real win for the Sanders camp. As the federation waited to endorse, one of its largest affiliates, the International Brotherhood of Electrical Workers, let its locals choose their own candidate. Dozens of them endorsed Bernie.[14]

The two-million-member Service Employees International Union (SEIU), a proponent of the Fight for $15, endorsed Hillary, despite Bernie's stronger position on income inequality and the minimum wage.[15] The State Employees Association of New Hampshire (SEIU) endorsed him nonetheless, because he "has always stood up for workers and the middle class," they said—as did the Vermont and other chapters of the National Education Association, the largest union in the country.[16]

Professional Staff Congress CUNY president Barbara Bowen was one of three in the forty-five-member AFT executive council who voted against the Clinton endorsement, even as her local was engaged in a bitter contract struggle.[17] As a former member of that union, which represents more than 27,000 faculty and graduate assistants at the City University of New York (CUNY), I followed its contract struggles and was aware of CUNY professors teaching in rat-infested classrooms without pay increases for years. Bernie urged New York governor Andrew Cuomo to offer a fair contract in a letter that was covered in the *New York Times* and other venues.[18] Citing CUNY's history, he pointed to the proven benefits of universal programs like free public higher education for working-class people and, throughout the campaign, he anchored his coalition-building efforts in policies aimed at improving their lives.

Policy

Trade

One of the fundamental differences between Bernie and Hillary regarded their views and political histories on US trade policy, and the Trans-Pacific Partnership (TPP) in particular. The TPP was a trade agreement involving the United States and eleven other countries along the Pacific Rim, in what would have been the world's largest free trade area, accounting for 40 percent of the global economy.

Obama positioned the TPP as his signature achievement and spent nearly his entire presidency negotiating it.

Hillary promoted free trade deals throughout her career and full-throatedly decried protectionism. She once praised the TPP as "the gold standard" and, in both her memoir and a widely cited *Foreign Policy* article, she argued forcefully for out-front US leadership in Asian Pacific markets. By positioning the TPP as a foreign policy imperative to counteract China's growing influence, both Obama and Hillary (as secretary of state) effectively removed trade from the domain of workforce and labor policy.

During the primary, progressive forces pressured Hillary to hold off on taking a position on the TPP, despite her vigorous embrace of Obama. Some of those forces derived from labor union solidarity on the issue, and some of them from Bernie's campaign. While standing at the Carrier plant in Indianapolis with workers about to lose their jobs to Mexico, Bernie hammered the point that unfettered "free trade" incentivizes companies to shut down manufacturing plants in the United States and move to Mexico, China, and other low-wage countries, where workers are paid a fraction of what they're paid here. He met with people around the country who had their lives torn apart by job-killing trade deals like the TPP. Tens of thousands of plants in the United States have been shut down and boarded up over the last fifteen to twenty years, and millions of decent-paying jobs have been lost. Once vibrant manufacturing towns now have sky-high poverty rates, massive home foreclosure, and (in some cases) major health crises and opioid addiction.

The TPP would have made the situation much worse. It promised to send American jobs offshore and put downward pressure on wages, and it threatened Internet freedoms and civil liberties, collective bargaining rights, public and environmental health, food safety, financial stability, and the sovereignty of our legal system. The TPP's Investor-State Dispute Settlement system would have made use of secret global tribunals to provide reparations to corporations if their future profits were limited by any government action—which bore stark contrast to meager reporting procedures for environmental, labor, and consumer violations. Plus, the deal involved eleven other countries and had no expiration date, which made it nearly impossible to repeal.

Hillary did take a position against the TPP, but it was late in the game, and by then, no one believed her, not even President Obama. In *Alter Egos*, Mark Landers wrote of Obama and Hillary that "when his aides told him that she had come out against the Trans-Pacific Partnership, the president merely rolled his eyes."[19]

College for All

One of the defining issues of the 2016 presidential race was the crisis in US higher education. Because of escalating costs, stagnant incomes, and a shift away from federal grants to marketized student loans, higher education has become increasingly difficult to access. Some people don't go to college because of the high costs, while others graduate with crippling debt. Such dynamics are part of the steady, decades-long retreat from the principle that providing for the general welfare is a fundamental role of government and should be among its highest priorities.

The assault on public higher education comes from several directions. Antisecular political conservatives would replace public schools at all levels with religious institutions. Privatizers see in this public good as in many others an opportunity for great profits by looting the public's resources. Other political reactionaries are threatened by the very idea of an educated citizenry and would rather roll back the clock to a time when access to higher education was restricted only to the children of the affluent.

Public higher education has become particularly vulnerable to this juggernaut in the aftermath of the financial crisis, as state governments continue to invoke fiscal stress to justify severe cuts in funding for public colleges and universities. In 1980, state governments contributed close to 80 percent of the cost of instruction. Now many students and their parents must bear more than half of that expense, and, in some states, twice as much. And they must do so on shrinking incomes.[20]

According to Kenneth Warren and Samir Sonti writing in the *Chronicle of Higher Education*, "Since the 1970s, tuition and fees at public institutions have increased by more than 350 percent, while pay for working- and middle-class households has stagnated." As a result, they add, "the cost of a public-college education accounts for almost 15 percent of the average family's annual income; 40 years ago it was 4 percent."[21] This affects a majority of college students in the United States, more than three-quarters of whom attend public institutions. It also calls into question the future of public higher education, as many public universities have planned significant budget cuts and downsizing into the future.

Outside of interest rate adjustments, expanded lending, and income-based repayment plans, the federal government has done little to address root causes. Pell Grants that used to cover three-quarters of the cost of a public college education for low-income students now cover just a third of it. The federal budget treats Pell Grants as discretionary spending, meaning that the program hangs in the balance each year until Congress decides how or whether to fund it. Many Republicans want to terminate the program entirely, and nearly all of them want to implement drastic funding reductions that would impact millions of low- and moderate-income students (and force many of them to drop out).[22]

Bernie's College for All Act made a powerful statement about the centrality of higher education as a public good— or, as he put it, "a right, not a privilege"—and offered an alternative to ensnaring masses of young people in debt prison and holding individuals and their families personally responsible for the skilling of the nation.

As a product of the US public higher education system myself (at CUNY and the University of Pittsburgh), I had firsthand experience of its benefits and challenges. A generation ago, US public colleges and universities were pathways of economic and social mobility for working-class students like me. Back in the 1970s, CUNY helped hundreds of thousands of students receive free higher education, many of them the first in their families to attend college. That changed in 1976 during the New York City fiscal crisis, a pivotal moment in the neoliberal turn toward public school retrenchment that Bernie was trying to reverse.

Clinton and her pundits openly rejected the concept of universal free public college, arguing that it gave the children of the wealthy, like Donald Trump's kids, a free ride on the backs of taxpayers. Her campaign made that claim even though our nation's wealthiest don't send their children to public schools, just as they don't use most public institutions.[23] Some on her side further argued that because dropout rates are high and rising, it would be a waste of taxpayer money for the government to subsidize free public college. What they failed to acknowledge is that many of those students drop out precisely *because* they can't afford it. As Sonti explained, "People aren't poor, as the reasoning so often proceeds, because they lack a college education; they lack a college education because they're poor."[24]

Clinton's plan for higher education involved catchphrases like Public–Private Partnerships, Innovation and Global Competitiveness, and developing untapped Human Capital to embellish her program of minimal government, private investment, and personal responsibility—or, in her crass vernacular, "skin in the game."[25] Her "New College Compact" included pooling outcome-contingent federal and state funds with inputs from individual families, and a student work requirement, presumably in either the public or private sector.[26] It positioned higher education as an engine of "global competitiveness," rather than as an institution for democratic citizen-making and a conduit of social solidarity.

Universal Health Care

Clinton's approach to health care was based on the same premises as her approach to higher education. Her agenda involved "improving upon" the Affordable Care Act (ACA) —which brought health care to 13 million Americans but left 28.5 million uninsured, most of them from low-income working families.[27] Bernie has been a highly visible advocate for single-payer health care for several decades. Similar to his arguments for universal higher education, he frequently talks about health care as a fundamental human right while pointing to other countries' systems as evidence of its viability.[28]

Appallingly, the United States is the only country in the industrialized world not to offer universal health care to its citizens, despite being the wealthiest country on earth. Instead, our government encourages corporations to mine life-or-death institutions for profits, similar to how other essential social services have been transformed into profitable industries.

The multibillion-dollar profiteering by pharmaceutical, insurance, and medical supply companies is legitimized by the prevailing orthodoxy in America that equates free markets with efficiency and choice, stresses individual responsibility, and offers only meager and highly conditional support for people when the bottom drops out.

The Clinton campaign, in sync with conservative politicians and corporate media, deployed teams of experts to attack Bernie on his health care plan and overall budget. Most of them offered the familiar austerity-driven refrain of "we can't afford it" or the technocratic critique that Bernie was offering "puppies and rainbows" rather than hard facts and analysis. Blogger-columnists Ezra Klein and Matt Yglesias were part of the latter chorus, with Klein attempting a kind of analytical takedown of Bernie's single-payer health care plan with claims that actually contradicted ones he'd made previously in favor of single-payer.[29] Yglesias's echo, published in the same venue (Vox.com) just twenty-four hours later, also called for more technical details and took a similarly sharp turn from his own arguments regarding the primacy of a candidate's vision and political principles over wonkish particulars.[30]

In September 2015, the *Wall Street Journal* published what journalist Doug Henwood calculated to be a "sensationalized tally" of Bernie's policy agenda, disparaging it as "the largest peacetime expansion of government in modern history."[31] Paul Krugman echoed the *Journal*'s assertion with his own austerity-minded critique of Bernie's health care plan, which, he alleged, had disingenuously inflated coverage and underestimated costs, and was virtually impossible to achieve politically.[32]

House minority leader Nancy Pelosi conceded that single-payer was popular among the American public, but in January 2015 she said that there was no use in discussing tax increases to support Bernie's plan because, she decided, "it's not going to happen."[33] A few days later, at a CNN town hall meeting, a member of the audience making $41,000 a year asked Bernie whether his health care plan would involve tax increases. Bernie explained that universal health care would mean more taxes, but that the cost would be more than offset by savings on health insurance premiums. The man affirmed that it was a trade-off that he'd be willing to accept.[34]

In February 2016, about ten days before the South Carolina primary, a foursome of retired chairs of the Council of Economic Advisers (CEA) who served under Presidents Obama and Clinton published an open letter to Bernie, likening his tax and budget proposals to the fiscal policy of irresponsible Republicans.[35] A group of economists and university faculty from our volunteer network helped to vet Bernie's economic plan. Not one of them suggested that his agenda was untenable, and most advised us to ignore Krugman and the CEA altogether. The Clintons, they pointed out, are masters at diverting what should be a public debate to one among wonks and beltway insiders, with the effect of using technocratic means to restrict the horizon of what's politically possible.

Bernie's budget sought to reverse the trend toward fiscal austerity and privatization with a series of policies that would raise taxes for the wealthy and substantially increase public spending. The plan was estimated to generate tens of millions of jobs, increase median income and average wages, reduce poverty to a third of its current rate, and, by 2024, eliminate the federal deficit.[36] Some of the economists in our network found his growth assumptions to be ambitious, but not overly so. Others rightly contended that social democratic reforms are predicated on the idea that capitalism can be fixed with public policy and regulation and thus fail to address profit motives and relations of exploitation. There were also constructive criticisms that his infrastructure plan could be better integrated with environmental policy, and one commenter offered the provocative suggestion that Bernie try to legislate a differential tax on profits that would increase if profits weren't reinvested in nonfinancial activity. They all pointed out, however, that even with more conservative growth assumptions, Bernie's New Deal would have vastly improved the living conditions of ordinary Americans.

In addition to single-payer health care, Bernie helped proliferate community health centers throughout the state of Vermont and around the country, and made them a centerpiece of his presidential campaign. Community health centers provide a range of health and wellness services to tens of millions of people, including medical, oral and dental, and mental health and substance abuse care. Some of them do much more by teaming up with local grocery stores, businesses, and service providers to offer a holistic, community-based model of healthy economic development. They serve hundreds of thousands of veterans; tens of thousands of homeless people; and millions of underserved seniors—regardless of a person's ability to pay.

Bernie tried to connect the dots between social class and health care during the primary by exposing the "hidden crisis" of dental care—not just the pain and suffering of untreated tooth decay, but the social stigma, which he has called a "badge of poverty."[37] The campaign also built upon his work as chairman of the Senate Subcommittee on Aging and the theme of "Poverty as a Death Sentence," with a town hall event at the Five Loaves and Two Fishes Food Bank in McDowell County, West Virginia. As of 2014,

35 percent of McDowell residents lived in poverty, nearly half of them children, just 6 percent of adults had a college education, and less than 66 percent graduated high school. The county had one of the lowest average life expectancies of men in the nation (sixty-four years), with suicides and drug overdoses as the leading causes of death. A six-hour car ride away, in Fairfax, Virginia, the average lifespan for a man was nearly twenty years longer (eighty-two years).[38] Just a few years prior to Bernie's visit, some 300,000 inhabitants of the state had been unable to drink or bathe in their water because of contamination from the Elk River chemical spill.[39]

During the campaign, Bernie visited other poor communities suffering from high unemployment and public health crises—in Puerto Rico, New York City, various Native American reservations—that had not been visited by a presidential candidate in decades, if ever.

Addressing the class dimension of the US health care crisis has also brought Bernie to confront powerful corporate interests in the pharmaceutical industry. That work dates back to when he was a congressman, when he organized direct action–style drug buying trips to Canada for women dependent on expensive breast cancer medicines. Trip participants saved an enormous amount of money, as women and older Vermonters were paying in some cases over 80 percent more than Canadians for their prescription drugs. Other congressmen followed suit and organized trips for their constituents.[40]

Big Pharma responded to the trips with claims that price controls would "stifle innovation."[41] But the real problem was that price controls would stifle profit-making. Behind skyrocketing drug prices—in some cases, by 5,000 percent overnight—are pharmaceutical giants who exploit sickness and vulnerability for enormous profit with the help of corrupt government officials from both major parties.[42] Tens of millions in campaign contributions and armies of high-paid lobbyists have bought drug companies in the United States a free hand in charging obscene prices for desperately needed treatments. People in other countries pay much lower prices for prescription drugs because their governments can negotiate a better deal for them. But pharmaceutical industry CEOs do not want the US government involved in setting drug prices because it would severely eat into their profits, bonuses, and compensation packages. Top industry CEOs make tens of millions per year in total compensation. And many of them stash their earnings in overseas tax havens and pay little to nothing in taxes.

Reining in Wall Street

Reining in Wall Street has been a centerpiece of Bernie's agenda, and rightly so, as the financial system constitutes the essential matrix through which the global economy now operates, and its tethers extend everywhere. It's a misnomer to use the term "deregulation" to describe what's happened over the last few decades, since that implies a diffusion or weakening of state control. It is important to remember that, despite the globalization of corporate power, the expansion and revamping of the global financial system over the last several decades occurred by the heavy hand of the US government, which remains the primary conductor of economic policy on a world scale.

Bernie has pushed for a long list of reforms aimed at using the federal government to rein in Wall Street excess. He's called for a modern-day Glass-Steagall to break up the big banks. And he wants to turn credit agencies into non-profits in order to prevent the corrupt practice of conferring triple-A ratings to toxic financial instruments. He targeted the "revolving door" that incentivizes regulators to give preferential treatment to some financial firms in hopes of sweet retirement deals. And he has argued against the Fed's "Jesse James guarding the banks" phenomenon, in response to JPMorgan Chase CEO Jamie Dimon's having served on the board of the New York Fed at the same time as his bank received an almost $400 billion bailout from it. Bernie played a major role in forcing an audit of the Federal Reserve after the Wall Street bailout, and he continues to push for audits to occur on an annual basis.

He also introduced legislation for a financial transactions tax (FTT) to help fund his College for All Act, which itself would help de-financialize US higher education by alleviating its reliance on marketized student loans.[43] He has also worked with the American Postal Workers Union to offer progressive banking alternatives to now prolific predatory lenders, whose business models hinge on churning profits from economic insecurity among poor and working-class people.[44]

Hillary tried to tarnish Sanders's record during the campaign by pointing to his yea vote for the Commodities Futures Modernization Act (CFMA), which deregulated the credit default swaps at the center of the financial crisis. Her attacks were entirely disingenuous, given that the CFMA was shoved deceitfully into an omnibus spending bill by Texas senator Phil Gramm during the lame duck session in the fog of the 2000 election recount. The legislation included a special exemption for energy derivative trading known as the "Enron loophole," named after the corrupt Texas-based energy company with which Gramm was closely associated—as was his wife, who *New York Times* opinion writer Bob Herbert described as "a demon for deregulation."[45] The CFMA was signed into law by President Bill Clinton.

Toward the end of the 2016 primary, the effects of wanton financial liberalization came to a head in Puerto Rico. As the island commonwealth teetered on the edge of default, hedge funds went on a feeding frenzy on the high-risk tax-exempt municipal bonds that the government was selling just to keep its schools and hospitals open. The territory was battling to salvage basic social services and institutions threatened by steep declines in their revenue base. As the situation worsened, hedge fund investors piled on, knowing full well that the territory and its inhabitants were in dire straits. When default became immanent, they sued Puerto Rico to avoid taking a haircut on their investments.[46]

The US Supreme Court put the territory's fate in the hands of Congress, many of whose election campaigns are funded by hedge fund managers. Obama's postfinancial crisis recovery had employed some Keynesian principles to stimulate job growth and rebound the economy.[47] But a different model was applied in Puerto Rico's "rescue"—one that involved punishing terms of structural adjustment in a region already beset by high unemployment, with over half of its children living in poverty.[48] Puerto Rico's "recovery" resembled that of the Troika's revanchist treatment of Greece, which, the IMF later admitted, likely destroyed the country's social infrastructure for years to come.[49]

During the campaign, Bernie visited the island and pushed back against structural adjustment by urging his fellow senators and Treasury Secretary Jack Lew to force the haircut that hedge fund managers were fighting. He introduced a bill to allow Puerto Rico to file for bankruptcy and receive emergency funds for a debt restructuring driven by local officials, and not by outsiders with a financial stake in the outcome. In his proposal, Puerto Ricans would be eligible for federal income and child tax credits, and access to health care and other social benefits would be improved.[50]

Bernie also called for measures to transition Puerto Rico's reliance on expensive imported oil to clean and locally produced energy sources, in light of its severe health and environmental problems, including those on the satellite island of Vieques. I visited both Vieques and Culebra in 2003 and wrote about the severe environmental aftereffects of the US Navy's occupation, including shockingly high cancer rates, live ordnance in the sea and on the beaches, and the destruction of sea and plant life. The Navy's postwar arrival brought land confiscations, job loss, and increased bombing exercises—with napalm and other chemical agents—that prompted waves of outward migration by a majority of the island's inhabitants. The number of half-built houses, town after town, grossly outnumbered the finished ones, caused in part by the Navy's abrupt retreat and decades of economic neglect and crisis.[51]

Anti-Imperialism

During the Democratic Party primary, much was made of the differential in foreign policy experience between Bernie and Hillary. Bernie countered that imbalance by questioning her judgment and pointing to his no vote on the widely unpopular Iraq War. He also distanced himself from her uncritical support for Benjamin Netanyahu's right-wing administration in Israel. Bernie was the only "A-list" presidential hopeful not to attend the annual meeting of the American Israel Public Affairs Committee (AIPAC), which he declined on account of his tight West Coast campaign schedule. One couldn't help but detect an echo of his boycott of Netanyahu's 2015 visit to Congress, however—as the speech he delivered that week broke with US government orthodoxy by recognizing Israel as an occupying force and stressing the political and humanitarian needs of Palestinians.

"We have to be a friend not only to Israel, but to the Palestinian people," he said, "where in Gaza, they suffer from an unemployment rate of 44 percent—the highest in the world—and a poverty rate nearly equal to that. There is too much suffering in Gaza to be ignored." He also spoke against the Israeli settlements and their devastating impact:

Right now, Israel controls 80 percent of the water reserves in the West Bank. Inadequate water supply has contributed to the degradation and desertification of Palestinian land. A lasting peace will have to recognize [that] Palestinians are entitled to control their own lives, and there is nothing human life needs more than water.[52]

In addition to bringing a class perspective to a conflict typically understood in religious and ethno-nationalist terms, he distanced himself from Hillary's notorious hawkishness in the Middle East. He met with Muslim leaders in mosques and Islamic societies and campaigned in Dearborn, Michigan, which houses the nation's largest Arab American population, and where he won 60 percent of the vote.[53] He was endorsed by the *Arab American News*, as well as by the first Muslim American congressman, Representative Keith Ellison, who Bernie appointed to the high-profile DNC Platform Drafting Committee, and eagerly promoted for DNC chair in 2017. He also worked closely with the Arab American Institute's James Zogby and appointed him to the DNC Platform Drafting Committee as well.

Bernie also went after Hillary on her relationship to Henry Kissinger—history's poster child for US imperialism. The day before the New Hampshire primary, my husband and I stopped by a Hillary campaign event in Manchester and watched in horror as Bill Clinton raved about his wife's close ties to Kissinger. We relayed the former president's remarks to the campaign's policy guru, Warren Gunnels, at a party after Bernie's epic win, and the three of us recalled together Kissinger's long list of war crimes. The next day Gunnels asked me to put together a "Top Ten" list on Kissinger's atrocities for the Milwaukee debate. In bed, nursing a hangover, I tapped out a "Top 13," with Greg Grandin's *Kissinger's Shadow* open on my pillow.

During the debate, when Hillary tried to corner him on foreign policy, Bernie came out swinging: "I am proud to say that Henry Kissinger is NOT my friend," he said angrily. "I will NOT take advice from Henry Kissinger." Hillary asked him from whom he *would* take advice. "Well, it ain't Henry Kissinger, that's for sure!" He then cited the millions of deaths in Vietnam, Cambodia, and elsewhere by Kissinger's hand. The next day Gunnels sent me a link to an *International Business Times* essay:

> Sanders' attack appeared to be pre-planned: Immediately after the exchange, his campaign sent out an email blast listing 13 controversial points of Kissinger's career, including his authorization of secret bombings in Laos and his help in planning CIA-led coups in South America.[54]

It was just one of a deluge of articles that day further exposing Kissinger's corporate-driven war crimes.

The standoff between Bernie's democratic socialism and establishment Democrats' agenda that played out during the 2016 presidential race is discussed in the upcoming chapters. Pundits and politicos continue to paper over such conflicts with claims that Hillary and Bernie's platforms differed only by degree, especially in the context of a Republican Party shifting further and further to the right. In Hillary's election postmortem, *What Happened*, for example, she characterizes Bernie's agenda as one driven by simple one-upmanship: to her $12 minimum wage he ran on a $15 wage, to her plan for tuition-free community college, he promoted free tuition for public college and universities, to her fixing of Obamacare, he called for Medicare for all.[55] That assessment perhaps willfully obscures the divergent class politics underlying their respective agendas, now decades in the making. The next chapter illuminates those critical differences by discussing how opportunistic Democrats associated with the Clinton campaign used the tensions and contradictions around race and gender politics in America to undermine Bernie's efforts to build a diverse class-conscious coalition. In doing so, they sharpened the contradictions around establishment democrats' apparent lip service to eradicating social inequality and neoliberal identity politics more generally.

3
The Campaign, Part 2:
Identity Politics

A month after Bernie announced his candidacy on the shores of Lake Champlain, he and former Maryland governor Martin O'Malley appeared at the 2015 Netroots Nation[1] conference in Phoenix, Arizona. During his talk, O'Malley was interrupted by protesters chanting, "What side are you on, my people?" and "Black Lives Matter!" A woman in a "Black Love" T-shirt took the stage, spoke about racist police violence, and asked the former governor how he would "dismantle structural racism in the United States." O'Malley talked policy, then, in an attempt to court the protesters, proclaimed "Black Lives Matter. White Lives Matter. All Lives Matter." The crowd erupted in boos and jeers. Perplexed, he repeated the mantra: "Black Lives Matter. White Lives Matter. *All Lives Matter*"—which only made matters worse.[2]

When Bernie appeared onstage, his talk was disrupted, too. Visibly annoyed, he responded that "black lives, of course, matter. I spent fifty years of my life fighting for civil rights and for dignity. But if you don't want me to be here, that's OK. I don't want to out-scream people."[3] A few weeks later, he was disrupted again by Black Lives Matter (BLM) activists in Seattle at a "Social Security Works" event organized to celebrate the eightieth anniversary of Social Security and the fiftieth anniversary of Medicare. It was a puzzling target for antiracist activism given the special importance of those programs to African American seniors and rigorous efforts of conservatives to defund and privatize them.[4] The crowd, some of them elderly, booed the activists for spoiling the occasion, to which the activists responded by accusing them of "white supremacist liberalism."[5]

Media coverage of the disruptions was ubiquitous and mixed. Within the movement, some activists viewed the disruptions as necessary to motivate Bernie to deepen his discussion of racial justice, while others called them counterproductive.[6] Critics suggested that the Seattle activists were agents provocateurs, pointing out that one of the young women had been a Sarah Palin supporter just a few years earlier. Others were disappointed by the activists' lack of sensitivity to the importance of Social Security and Medicare for working-class people from all backgrounds. Historian Touré Reed, for example, described the intervention as "somewhere between arrogant (she represents no constituency to speak of) and politically misguided—many black lives, including both of my grandmothers', have benefited greatly from Social Security, Medicare, and Medicaid for decades."[7]

I agreed with Reed that the attack on Bernie in the name of antiracism was misplaced, not just because I know him, but because the move appeared to be aimed at controlling the microphone as an end in itself—what African American studies historian Robin Kelley described as a "politics of recognition"—rather than one driven by a politics rooted in a social democratic or anticapitalist vision.[8] There was also the problem of young activists claiming to speak on behalf of "the black community," which itself is an abstract term that obscures class and power inequalities among black Americans; since victories of the 1960s and '70s, inequality has advanced to such a degree that it is today much higher than that among white Americans.[9] It also seemed antithetical to what Left, or even progressive, politics require, which is coalition-building that's principled, yet inclusive and extensive enough to confront elite power (or at least unite around programs like Social Security).

Bernie has not been a member of the Senate committees that directly shape US criminal justice policy, but he often cites the United States' obscene, racially disparate incarceration rates when arguing for a radical redistribution of political and economic power. He is mortified by the 50 percent unemployment rate among black youth, and he has tried to use the various legislative tools at his disposal to create jobs for young people. His approach is consistent with that of civil rights leaders like A. Philip Randolph and Bayard Rustin,[10] who viewed public investment and full employment as engines of mobility, dignity, and racial justice.

Regardless of Bernie's political views and history, the

O'Malley and Clinton camps seized the opportunity to paint the senator "from the white state of Vermont" as focusing too narrowly on the economy and lacking experience on issues of specific concern to black and female voters. That was despite O'Malley and Clinton's own egregious records on racial profiling and racist policies behind mass incarceration.[11]

That summer, I was working with the campaign to organize surrogates, and at the time of the disruptions, I received a letter from University of Pennsylvania professor Adolph Reed, Jr., offering to help. Reed, Jr., is a distinguished scholar of race and racism, known for his blistering critiques of Senator Obama's rhetoric of the "underclass" (recall for instance Obama's invocation of "Cousin Pookie"), when most of his peers were caught up in the exuberance of the first black president.[12] We tossed around the idea of putting together a letter signed by black intellectuals to counteract the race-baiting, but we reasoned that it would play too much like crass identity politics. Instead, we organized a consortium of Left and progressive intellectuals around the concept of higher education as a public good—called "Higher Ed for Bernie"—and we worked to explain how universal free college could help mitigate racial disparities in US social institutions.

Cornel West was among the first we invited to the initiative. West had fast become a vital force in the campaign, appealing directly to people's sense of injustice and morality and inviting audiences to join Bernie's "Love Train." Reed, Jr., also published a lengthy article (an interview) on the relationship between race and class politics in the context of the campaign, as did Touré Reed, who placed Bernie and the BLM activists who protested him within the long history of liberals' delinking of racial disparities from class inequality.[13]

The campaign itself responded by meeting with anti-racist activists, hiring more staff for outreach to black and Latino voters, and working with high-profile black and Latino surrogates. They also added policy proposals on institution-based racial disparities to his stump speech and highlighted his civil rights history, including his participation in the 1963 March on Washington, an arrest for civil disobedience against school segregation, and direct involvement in the Congress of Racial Equality and Student Nonviolent Coordinating Committee.

Importantly, the campaign also put forth a comprehensive civil rights and criminal justice policy platform to combat the use of state violence against communities of color and what Bernie called "the militarization of police," whose behavior he likened to an "occupying army."[14] His agenda sought to address injustices in the legal system that were robbing people of their right to due process, and it opposed mandatory minimums held over from the war on drugs that have resulted in severe sentencing disparities among racial groups. He prioritized voting rights and called for the re-enfranchisement of the some two million African Americans who have had their right to vote taken away by a felony conviction. And he denounced the racist stereotyping of black youth as "thugs" and "superpredators."

As the campaign progressed, efforts to foster a more racially diverse, class-conscious coalition brought Bernie to places that establishment Democrats typically avoid. He was the only 2016 presidential candidate to visit Indian reservations, including South Dakota's Pine Ridge, the historic site of the Wounded Knee Massacre and American Indian Movement activism. In Yakima, Washington, 7,000 people turned out to see him at a campaign rally—the first time in over a decade that a presidential candidate visited there. The event opened with a prayer for ethnic and racial unity and a performance by the all-female White Swan dancers, some not more than five years old. His appeal among Native American communities was in part based on his vehement opposition to the Dakota Access Pipeline at Standing Rock, Keystone XL, and other pipelines affecting Native American lands. But it also had to do with his commitment to eradicating poverty through addressing problems of joblessness, public health, and education, of particular concern to those living on reservations.

Bernie also visited poor communities in Puerto Rico as well as New York. MSNBC's Lawrence O'Donnell ran a story in April 2016 on New York City's housing projects featuring Ritchie Torres, a councilman representing one of the city's poorest districts. O'Donnell helped to publicize a letter that Torres sent to all of the presidential candidates inviting them to tour Public Housing Authority buildings to see for themselves what decades of public divestment does to communities. Clinton visited the Corsi Houses in East Harlem, and Sanders toured the Howard Houses in Brownsville. After his tour, the campaign released a national affordable housing platform that incorporated Torres's suggestions, in addition to plans to address leaky roofs, mold, heating, vermin, and broken elevators. Torres endorsed him soon after, explaining that "Bernie represents a special phenomenon in progressive politics. He singularly has made inequality and poverty the focal point of the presidential election."[15] Torres also stated in interviews that no presidential candidate in recent history had visited Brownsville.

Despite these and other efforts, the problem of how to confront racial and gender inequality and how to organize among specific racial and ethnic groups continued to loom over the campaign. That was especially true in the lead-up to the races in Nevada and South Carolina—which boast large Hispanic and African American populations, respectively, and which were promoted widely as Clinton's impenetrable "firewall."

Nevada and South Carolina

We now know from WikiLeaks that in the days before the caucuses in Nevada—where Latinos make up 28 percent of the population—DNC chairman Tom Perez recommended to the Clinton campaign that it combine austerity and identity politics to paint Bernie as the candidate of young white liberals. By asserting that Bernie's single-payer and immigration policies were not immediately passable into law, Perez argued, Hillary could render her rival as tone-deaf to the particular needs of black and Latino voters who were living in a state of emergency.[16]

Chairman of the Congressional Hispanic Caucus representative Luis Gutiérrez, secretary of housing and urban development Julian Castro, and civil rights organizer

Dolores Huerta joined in the pile-on. Gutiérrez issued particularly manic attacks on Bernie's guest worker policies, saying they were "straight from the Republican anti-immigration playbook."[17] Progressive Caucus co-chairman representative Raúl Grijalva called Gutiérrez's claims "disingenuous" and challenged his House colleague to a public discussion on the candidates' records.[18]

It was true that Bernie worked with Republicans on immigration policy. During the Wall Street bailout, the big banks laid off over 100,000 US workers while hiring cheaper labor abroad. Bernie collaborated with Senator Chuck Grassley to prohibit corporations receiving bailout funds from laying off Americans and replacing them with lower paid guest workers. He also tried to prevent Fortune 500 companies from outsourcing US jobs or transforming them into part-time, temporary ones. And he managed to pass an amendment for a youth jobs program, which would have disproportionately helped black and Latino youths. Such measures, supported by various labor unions and the AFL-CIO,[19] were meant to prevent Silicon Valley billionaires, such as Bill Gates and Mark Zuckerberg, from placing workers from other countries in precarious working conditions and pitting foreign- and native-born against each other to ultimately drive down wages *for all workers*. The Clinton campaign, by contrast, was considering Gates to be Hillary's running mate.[20]

As Grijalva correctly noted, the allegations from Gutiérrez and others that Bernie's empathy extended only to "white workers" were nothing short of disingenuous. After all, Bernie's campaign platform on immigration called for increasing the number of refugees welcomed in the United States each year, passing the DREAM Act and creating a pathway to citizenship for undocumented people, and cracking down on workplace exploitation. Bernie's repeated calls for an increase in the minimum wage would especially help working-class immigrants, many of whom work in the lowest paid industries in the United States. He also wanted to make it easier for them to join labor unions and bargain for better wages and working conditions, in addition to his out-front opposition to free trade agreements, such as the North American Free Trade Agreement (NAFTA) and the Central America Free Trade Agreement, that have been downright ruinous for large numbers of workers in Mexico and Central America.

As part of an effort to expose the plight of immigrant laborers in the United States, the Bernie campaign aired a video, really a mini-documentary, on the Coalition of Immokalee Workers in Florida. The video highlighted how immigrant farm workers are being ruthlessly exploited by large corporations in the food industry and the necessity for worker-led labor organizing campaigns to confront such abuses. Bernie visited Immokalee back in 2008 and witnessed firsthand the workers' horrific working conditions —what he described as "the lowest economic rung" of the race to the bottom. After his visit, he organized a Senate hearing on the conditions surrounding tomato pickers in Florida's farm fields and waged a campaign to pressure Burger King and the Florida Tomato Growers Exchange to agree to the Immokalee coalition's reform program. Bernie's efforts helped to raise the coalition's national profile, and a few years later it was able to secure agreements for wage increases, safety standards, and a code of conduct regarding wage theft and verbal and sexual abuses.

In addition to focusing on the workplace, Bernie's immigration reform platform also called for ending the overmilitarization of US borders, providing immigrants legal counsel and due process in the criminal justice system, eradicating "bed quotas" for US Immigration and Customs Enforcement, and ending arbitrary family deportation sweeps. He also introduced legislation to ban the use of private prisons, which are now playing a key role in the Trump administration's hardline approach to immigration (which includes plans to end the practice of "catch and release" and increase the number of jails for undocumented people). Private prison companies were major donors to Trump's campaign and have sunk millions into lobbying for immigration reform. When Trump was elected president, private prison companies like the GEO Group saw their stock prices soar, in some cases by more than 100 percent.[21]

More consequential than Castro and Gutiérrez's defamations, however, was former majority leader Senator Harry Reid's intervention in Nevada. In 2008, Hillary suffered an embarrassing third-place defeat in Iowa but managed to eke out a victory in New Hampshire. This time, in 2016, she won Iowa by just two-tenths of a percent—a virtual tie and, for her, an abysmal showing, given that Bernie was polling at just 5 percent in national polls at the start of the race. Hillary was predicted to lose New Hampshire by double digits, but no one expected such an epic shellacking. He not only beat her by a gaping margin (60 percent to 38 percent), but he won the most votes ever in the state's primary—31 percent more than the previous record-setter.[22]

Those historic wins gave Bernie enormous momentum going into Nevada. So much so that they apparently inspired Harry Reid to call D. Taylor, president of the Las Vegas local of the Culinary Workers Union, to get him to mobilize his workers to caucus for Hillary—after both leaders had publicly declared their neutrality. Reid also called casino executives on the Strip, a Clinton stronghold, to ensure that their workers had time off to participate. All six casino caucuses favored Clinton. "Nevada could indeed prove to be the contest that saved Clinton's campaign," as *USA Today* put it.[23] Though Bernie lost Nevada, he did win the majority of Latino votes.[24] Contrary to what establishment Democrats had wagered with their attacks on Bernie's immigration record, polls showed that reform at the border was less important to Hispanic voters in 2016 than issues of college affordability, health care, and income fairness.[25]

The dynamic in South Carolina, and throughout the South, was markedly different. Hillary was far ahead in the polls, and her camp's presence in the region was much stronger. That summer, South Carolinians were mourning the police murder of Walter Scott and the heinous massacre of churchgoers at Emanuel AME by a twenty-one-year-old white supremacist. Bernie was deeply concerned about racial profiling, hate groups, and the increased militarization of police forces in America. And he wanted to connect the dots between racial injustice and economic inequality and to expose the powerful interests working to divide and conquer poor and working-class Americans. But his campaign organization in South Carolina, and much of the South, was far too weak to move the electoral dial in any meaningful way.

One of Bernie's earliest campaign trips to the South involved his July 2015 appearance at the 57th National Convention of the Southern Christian Leadership Conference Gala and the Democratic Party Jefferson-Jackson dinner, both in Louisiana. He had planned to visit Charleston, South Carolina, soon after, but canceled the trip out of respect for the victims of the Emanuel AME Church massacre. I recall these events clearly; it was around that time that I started writing research memos for the campaign and content for his online media outlet, *Democracy Daily*. For his rescheduled visit to Charleston in August, I prepared background materials on criminal justice and predatory lending in South Carolina. What I found was deeply disturbing.

In South Carolina, where the African American population is one of the largest in the country, the banking industry is wreaking havoc with subprime mortgages and other nefarious financial schemes, targeting those least able to fight back: the poor, immigrants, the disabled, and the elderly. The number of predatory lending institutions nationwide rivals that of Starbucks outlets, but they are heavily concentrated in the South. South Carolina boasts one of the highest foreclosure rates in the country, and its inhabitants continue to suffer the effects of stagnant or shrinking incomes.[26] Those considered high credit risks rely on cocktails of shady financial products, like rapid refunds, and car and payday loans, with annual percentage rates as high as 400 percent. Despite marketers' claims that the loans are for emergencies, most borrowers use them to cover daily living expenses, like rent and utilities.

Clinton made her views on predatory lending clear during a 2007 speech at NASDAQ headquarters in the lead-up to the financial crisis: "Now these economic problems are certainly not all Wall Street's fault—not by a long shot … Homebuyers who paid extra fees to avoid documenting their income should have known they were getting in over their heads."[27] Working-class and fixed-income homeowners in South Carolina, most of them African American, were apparently more to blame for their devastating losses in 2008 than the Wall Street bankers who used their homes as poker chips. Nonetheless, her campaign used the recurring talking point that Bernie's attacks on Wall Street elites were "tone-deaf" to the specific needs of people of color.

Those kinds of attacks on Bernie intensified as the South Carolina primary drew closer, especially when he began to attract black and Latino surrogates with significant name recognition. National Association for the Advancement of Colored People (NAACP) past president Ben Jealous endorsed Bernie a few days before the primary in New Hampshire, where he delivered a moving personal reflection on his interracial background and the struggles of poor and working-class people on both sides of the color line.[28] Former Ohio State senator Nina Turner broke with establishment Democrats to support Bernie and became a popular spokeswoman for the campaign and, later, president of Our Revolution.

Erica Garner, the daughter of the New York man who

was killed in a police chokehold, released a widely viewed video in support of the campaign's efforts toward criminal justice reform and recounted her tragic story at campaign events in South Carolina.[29] Stars like Danny Glover and Spike Lee appeared with him in commercials and at rallies, and Harry Belafonte, himself a beneficiary of the GI Bill, said that Bernie represented a "certain kind of truth that's not often evidenced in the course of politics."[30] Seattle Seahawks defensive end Michael Bennett pledged his vote on TV, naming social justice and climate control as key issues.[31]

A handful of rappers expressed their support as well, including Scarface, Bun B, Big Boi, Lil B, Swae Lee and Slim Jxmmi of Rae Sremmurd, and Killer Mike, one of the campaign's strongest surrogates. Communications guru Michael Briggs told me that the campaign found out about Killer Mike from his tweets about the senator's work on voting rights. Briggs was present at their highly publicized first meeting at Atlanta's Busy Bee Cafe and described it as "comfortable and organic," despite the unlikely pairing. Killer Mike said it was "just a conversation between two angry radical guys, one 74 and white, one 40 and black, finding common ground."[32] At the rally afterward, he told the crowd that he was for Bernie "because working-class and poor people deserve a chance at economic freedom and yes, if you work 40 hours a week, you should not be in poverty."[33]

Despite Bernie's growing popularity, African American politicians stayed the course with Clinton and doubled down on her delinking of race politics from its class dimensions. South Carolina's much revered Democratic congressman

James Clyburn endorsed Clinton on MSNBC and said of Sanders's education platform: "I do not believe there are any free lunches. And certainly there's not going to be any free education."[34] The comment was remarkably similar to one made earlier in the primary season by Jeb Bush in response to queries about how he planned to appeal to black voters: "Our message is one of hope and inspiration. It isn't one of division and get in line and we'll take care of you with free stuff."[35] Clyburn and Bush's remarks echoed Milton Friedman's 1977 book, *There's No Such Thing as a Free Lunch.*[36]

Civil rights icon Representative John Lewis turned up the volume when he denigrated Sanders's history of civil rights activism during the Congressional Black Caucus PAC's public endorsement of Hillary Clinton:

> Well, to be very frank ... I never saw him, I never met him ... I'm a chairman of the Student Nonviolent Coordinating Committee for three years, from 1963 to 1966. I was involved in the sit-ins, the freedom rides, the March on Washington, the march from Selma to Montgomery ... But I met Hillary Clinton. I met President Clinton.

That same week, *Time* magazine published a vulgar hit piece questioning the authenticity of a photo of Bernie leading a sit-in against segregated housing.[37]

A storm of criticism followed Lewis's remarks, including those who pointed out that in 1964, Hillary was canvassing for ultra-conservative Barry Goldwater, an opponent of the Civil Rights Act.[38] Others took offense at Lewis's insinuation that low-profile organizers in the civil rights movement didn't count. Lewis walked back his claims, but when questioned by journalists about Bernie's platform, he reverted to Friedmanism:

> There's not anything free in America. We all have to pay for something. Education is not free. Health care is not free. Food is not free. *Water is not free* [emphasis added]. I think it's very misleading to say to the American people, we're going to give you something free.[39]

Clyburn and another Democratic congressman, Cedric Richmond from Louisiana, also charged that Bernie's plan for free public higher education would undercut historically black colleges and universities (HBCUs), even though half of them are public.[40] Policy guru Warren Gunnels explained to *USA Today* that Bernie's higher education proposals would make public HBCUs tuition-free, and at private ones, students would have lower student loan interest rates, and triple the number of work study opportunities, in addition to a $30 billion fund to support private, nonprofit HBCUs.[41]

What was alarming about Clyburn was not his misrepresentation of Bernie's position on HBCUs, but his willingness to elevate the interests of a small, historically black university (he sits on the board of Allen University) above the ability of *all* black students to pursue higher education without constraint by ability to pay.[42] His and Lewis's rejection of higher education as a public good—not just as an attack on Bernie, but *in principle*—threw a bright spotlight on establishment Democrats' practice of branding its conservative class politics as racial justice.

Clinton won by a landslide in South Carolina, prompting increased criticism that Bernie's campaign had not adequately taken stock of the specific needs of black voters. In response, African American studies professor Cedric Johnson published a Q&A-type essay, which began with the rhetorical question "Why did black people vote against their interests?" That was not how Bernie saw it, but no doubt some of his supporters did. Johnson swiped that kind of thinking aside, asserting that "black people are not a herd of sheep, and this is a notion that many folks, including some blacks, need to disabuse themselves of."[43]

Black voters in South Carolina and elsewhere, Johnson pointed out, *did* vote their interests, *as they themselves saw them*. Some people appreciated Clinton's experience, pragmatism, and/or her embrace of Obama; others were excited by the prospect of the first woman president. And certainly people inside the Democratic Party stood to gain from siding with her camp, from jobs to government contracts to political access, and other aspects of the Clintons' deep patronage networks.

What Adolph Reed, Jr., and I witnessed on the ground in South Carolina was an almost religious devotion to Obama, with some viewing Bernie's popularity among young people as a threat to the president's legacy.[44] There was also palpable fear of a Trump victory and conviction that Hillary would fare better in the general election. In the context of a deeply conservative state, Clinton's claims that policies like single-payer and free college were untenable and "pie in the sky," echoed by trusted surrogates like Clyburn and Lewis, were understandably persuasive.

At a breakfast gathering for campaign volunteers at Lizard's Thicket (where "Country Cookin' Makes Ya Good

Lookin'"), locals expressed the need for more door knock-
ing and better messaging on how Bernie was positioned to
win. They, and we, were coming up against the fact of Hillary's firewall, built over the course of decades. By early
November, her machine said that it had contacted more than
142,000 unique voters and held 1,100 grassroots organizing
events across the state.[45] To hit those marks, Bernie would
have had to start much earlier and put together a tighter
organization. Even then, a win was not likely.

One night, campaign staffer (and comrade) Lawrence
Moore brought Reed and me to the town of Aiken to talk
about the campaign at the local Democratic Party's weekly
meeting. Reed gave a short speech on Bernie's platform,
after which we took questions from the thirty-plus person
audience. A black woman in her mid-fifties asked him
how "a white senator" from "the white state of Vermont"
could understand the problems she faced. We'd heard that
several times before—about Bernie and about Vermont. He
responded by rattling off Bernie's policy agenda: "expanding Social Security, increasing minimum wage, free college
and health care, fair lending ..." Then he turned to her and
respectfully asked, "Which one of these wouldn't be good
for us?" That seemed to make sense to her and others.

But at the end of the day, it wasn't enough. It wasn't
that the campaign didn't speak to issues of specific concern
to South Carolina's black voters. It most certainly did. It
was that because of having gone "all in" in Iowa and New
Hampshire, for understandable strategic reasons, and
playing catch-up in Nevada as the race tightened, the campaign simply came late to the game in South Carolina and

did not have a chance to perform the necessary outreach and groundwork to explain how his policies would work for the black working class.

In South Carolina, Bernie lost to Clinton among black voters by an enormous margin: 86 percent to 14 percent. That margin was slimmer when disaggregated by age, as 62 percent of South Carolina's black voters under age thirty went for Clinton, while 38 percent did for Sanders.[46] As the race progressed, Bernie's popularity among black voters improved significantly with expanded outreach and name recognition. Polls had Clinton dominating Michigan just a few weeks after South Carolina, but he pulled a major upset in the state and won it with a much larger share of the vote among African Americans.[47]

An NBC News analysis of twenty-five states that held primaries, and where exit polls were conducted, found that black voters under age thirty favored Bernie over Clinton, 52 percent to 47 percent. Those voters, NBC explained, did not turn out in large enough numbers to tip in his favor.[48] A more recent, 2017 Harvard-Harris poll found that Bernie was the most popular active politician in America—viewed favorably among 73 percent of African Americans, 68 percent of Hispanics, and 62 percent of Asian Americans.[49]

Gender

The 2016 primary also exposed contradictions around gender politics among Democrats, against the backdrop of a possible first woman president and ongoing virulent attacks on reproductive rights by conservatives. Clinton had the résumé, and she had spent a lifetime preparing to run for president, including a run in the 2008 Democratic Party primary when she won eighteen million votes, or, as she put it, "18 million cracks in the glass ceiling."[50] But while members of the Democratic Party establishment including Planned Parenthood, NOW, Emily's List, and NARAL all lined up behind her, Clinton was not able to secure the support of many progressive feminists and a large majority of women millennials.

Such fissures within the so-called "woman vote" spurred a variety of reactions from liberal feminists in the Hillary camp. Surrogates like Gloria Steinem patronized Bernie's millennial supporters on the basis of their age, claiming that they only chose him because "that's where the boys were"—a stunning yet telling reaction by one of America's most iconic feminists.[51] First female secretary of state Madeleine Albright resorted to downright scolding: "there's a special place in hell for women who don't help each other," she remarked.[52] (One wonders what the mothers of the half million Iraqi children who died as a result of Albright's sanctions thought of that—sanctions that Albright defended as "worth the price."[53])

Female members of the media went even further. MSNBC's Joy Reid lost it over Bernie supporters throwing dollar bills at Hillary's limo en route to a lavish fund-raiser at actor George Clooney's house. Reid painted the activists' move as a transgression against all women by likening it to throwing dollars at a strip club. She juxtaposed the story with an event the week before in which a Bernie surrogate called Clinton a "corporate whore." In an interview with *Washington Post* reporter Abby Phillip, Reid pleaded, "Has the Democratic race gone over the edge?" Instead of addressing the actual content of the activists' critique of campaign finance, Phillip claimed that Bernie supporters were frustrated by his lack of a "path forward" and "strongly dislike Secretary Clinton *on a personal level.*"[54]

Cries of sexism also rang from the pages of the typically more progressive outlet, the *Nation*, with writers Katha Pollitt and Joan Walsh echoing the Clinton talking point that Bernie's campaign was "one-note" and not responsive to the particular needs of female voters. Walsh was especially tweaked about the so-called Bernie-bro phenomenon and repeatedly cast Bernie's campaign as a cult of angry white men. The *Nation* also featured essays from writers like Liza Featherstone, whose "Why This Socialist Feminist Is Not Voting for Hillary" laid out the core principles of socialist feminism in sharp contrast to those associated with Clinton's corporate "lean-in" feminism.

For Featherstone, socialist feminism "assumes that redistribution is the best way to begin improving life for the vast majority of women, both materially and socially."[55] Such a politics, articulated in the call for the March 2017 Women's Strike, combines struggles against sexism, homophobia, and xenophobic immigration policies with those addressing wage and workplace inequality, lack of access to education and health care, and matters of war and aggression—in other words, it accounts for inequalities of class.[56] "Corporate feminism" on the other hand, or what Facebook CEO Sheryl Sandberg termed "lean-in feminism," focuses on individual success and mobility within a system driven by exploitation and economic inequality. If individual women work hard and set their sights high, they too can have it all, just like the men. The poor can stay poor, and the rich can stay rich, just as long as "the 1 percent" is made more diverse.

During the campaign, I wrote a few essays aimed at demonstrating how Bernie's policies were more "pro-woman" than Hillary Clinton's. Bernie has supported women's right to choose, unequivocally. The Clinton campaign rightly put reproductive rights up-front in 2016, but historically Clinton herself has talked about abortion in stigmatizing terms, arguing that it must be "safe, legal and rare."[57] Bernie helped lead the opposition to GOP efforts to cut the Women, Infants, and Children (WIC) program, which provides nutrition assistance for new and expecting mothers and their babies. Clinton supported nutrition programs as well, but in 1996, she openly backed her husband's agenda to "end welfare as we know it," which effectively reduced welfare rolls but skyrocketed the number of people living in extreme poverty.

Both candidates called for pay equity and paid family leave, but Bernie consistently has called for increasing the minimum wage to $15, which would disproportionately benefit women workers, especially those who work for tips. Clinton supported an increase to $12, but what really damned her, at least in progressives' eyes, were her ties to Wall Street and companies like Walmart—the object of a major sex-discrimination lawsuit brought to the Supreme Court by a million and a half female workers. Clinton served on the giant retailer's board for years, and in 2016 the

Hillary Victory Fund received a $353,400 donation from Walmart heiress Alice Walton.[58]

Even with good wages, many Americans continue to spiral into bankruptcy from excessive medical costs. Women are especially afflicted, because we are less likely than men to be insured, and our health care expenses tend to be higher. During the campaign, Clinton said that she would go with "what works" in Obamacare, but Bernie's "Medicare for All" would have gone much further to reduce out of pocket costs for poor and working-class women. Clinton was also reticent to oppose the Trans-Pacific Partnership (TPP) and has been a major supporter of free trade agreements like NAFTA for much of her career. Trade is not often viewed as a woman's issue, but in fact it is. The TPP promised to create jobs in the developing world, but they were mostly the kind that exploit poor women. Women in the United States also stood to lose, because the TPP would have let corporations outsource low-wage majority-woman jobs (and some high-wage ones, too).[59] And while Bernie called for tuition-free college for all so that poor and working-class kids could access higher education, Clinton's higher education policy (as outlined in Chapter 2) required that young people have "skin in the game."

Hillary sold her rejection of policies like free college and single-payer as a woman's pragmatism in a world where women must perform twice as well. It's often true that we must, but that doesn't make Hillary's policies good for all women. As literary theorist Walter Benn Michaels said during an interview on his provocative book *The Trouble with Diversity*: "You know you live in a world that loves neoliberalism when having some people of color who are rich is supposed to count as good news for all the people of color who are poor."[60] The same could be said for versions of feminism that exploit women's sense of purported biological unity and common experiences of patriarchy in order to paint elite women's successes as universal wins—instead of fighting for material equality with men *and among women.*

Race, Class, Gender

Prejudice based on race, gender, age, and other ascriptive features requires serious attention in America today. Racial insensitivity and acts of bias continue to infect workplaces, college campuses, and other social institutions and are proliferating with the ascendancy of reactionary forces associated with the Trump presidency. Denouncing racist and sexist underclass mythologies proffered by both major political parties, and educating publics on historical and current forms of stereotyping, discrimination, and hate in America, can go a long way in changing perceptions and institutional cultures. The Sanders campaign could have done a better job of taking up that charge early on.

But solving problems of racial, ethnic, and gender-based disparity in our social and political institutions is going to require much more than consciousness raising. As Hillary herself put it to BLM activists when they asked her how she was going to change "white hearts," "Look, I don't believe you change hearts. I believe you change laws, you change allocation of resources, you change the way systems operate. You're not going to change every heart. You're not."[61]

Hillary was right. In capitalist society, all politics is a class politics. Assuming that an essential unity or "community" exists within particular racial, ethnic, and gender categories risks obscuring class hierarchies and relations of exploitation among people *within* such groupings.

Historically, racism and sexism have operated as generative forces in capitalist social relations. Various forms of racial, ethnic, and gender ideologies have been, and are, deployed to exploit and subjugate whole populations of people through social processes that inscribe them into hierarchies based on how they appear. Such processes—from segregated schools and housing to the use of "science" to distinguish populations by physical traits—help to normalize hierarchies of status and wealth by making them appear natural or common sense.[62]

There is no biological justification for racial hierarchies or essential unities among racial and gender groups, however. Processes of racialization have changed over time and across populations, from the contrivances of race science and eugenics in the late nineteenth and early twentieth centuries, to the racist tiering of New Deal social benefits, to more contemporary forms of stigmatization through the use of slurs like "welfare queens," "superpredators," and "Cousin Pookie."[63] Race and gender politics in America have changed, too, including major shifts in the class structuring of American society brought by the feminist and civil rights movements and the shattering of glass ceilings in corporate board rooms and the Forbes 400.

Over the last forty years, free market policy has been lauded by political elites—from Reagan to Obama—as

The Answer to our societal woes. Yet governmental programs aimed at providing basic social protections for all, without caveat, may offer the most effective means for combatting racial and gender disparities and building popular institutional bases for addressing bigotry and bias.[64] Certainly that was the vision of major civil rights leaders such as Bayard Rustin, Dr. Martin Luther King, Jr., and A. Philip Randolph, whose agendas combined racial and economic justice and promoted them for all.

Randolph, in particular, positioned black workers as protagonists of civil rights, and sought to merge movements for black freedom with the general struggle of "the common man."[65] In 1966, he published "A Freedom Budget for All Americans," which offered a concrete policy agenda for reducing unemployment and poverty through increasing the federal minimum wage to a living wage; guaranteeing income for those unable to work; promoting universal access to quality housing, proper medical care, and higher education; improving the country's infrastructure and public transportation system; and raising environmental standards.

As US politics took a conservative turn in the late 1970s and 1980s, so did the course of race and gender politics. Programs of full employment, universal health care and education, and other forms of investment in public goods were supplanted by emphases on personal responsibility and upward mobility, and, for feminism and civil rights, equal access and participation in consumer society.[66] Cornel West remarked on such developments in an interview with Chris Hedges: "What took the place of collective fightback was individual outward upward mobility," West lamented;

"moral conviction" got replaced with "ruthless ambition."[67] He was referring to the historical formation of a black professional managerial class[68] and the work of some members of the Congressional Black Caucus,[69] whose interests during the 2016 primary tended to align more neatly with Hillary Clinton, the neoliberal political elite, than with Bernie Sanders, the democratic socialist.

Barbara Ehrenreich made a similar point about "glass ceiling" feminism in her work on domestic labor.[70] She went so far as to pass herself off as a Merry Maid in order to write firsthand about how the well-heeled hire immigrant women to clean their homes because they themselves are "above" housework and too busy to raise their own children. In the struggle over housework, she concluded, what amounted to a victory for some women did not translate as a victory for all of them—in fact, quite the opposite.

Reed further clarified such dynamics in an email exchange with me in the days leading up to the South Carolina primary:

> Claims of common interest based on shared racial identity is itself an expression of a class politics, the politics of the professional and managerial strata that formed the basis of the new black political elite. That's who has an interest in denying or submerging class dynamics among black Americans.

He and others like Cedric Johnson have argued that black poverty and unemployment, and racial disparities in criminal justice and other social institutions, involve racism and discrimination but are not reducible to them. They must be understood, rather, in broad terms, as products of structural dynamics in the political economy.[71] It is on the basis of political economy, therefore, that strategies to eradicate racial and gender inequality should be formulated.

For Bernie, that has meant challenging some of the basics of American capitalism, like exploitation, profit motives, corporate power, and ruling class ideology—including ideologies of gender and racial superiority—that the bipartisan political establishment continues to facilitate and legitimize. Like Randolph's "A Freedom Budget for All Americans," Bernie's political framework involves combining the programs of civil and economic rights by way of social wage policies aimed at empowering working people of all races, genders, sexualities, and nationalities—instead of replicating the "divide and conquer" that buoys the ruling class.

4

The Convention, the General Election, and Its Aftermath

As the Democratic Party primary advanced through the spring, Bernie's disappointing loss to Hillary in New York signaled a significant narrowing of his campaign's path forward. But even after the very last contest in Washington, DC, he did not immediately concede the nomination. In the afterglow of an unexpectedly impactful campaign, third party activists and some progressives called for him to re-enter the race as a third party candidate. The campaign itself entertained the possibility of staying in and trying to flip superdelegates, since by then Bernie had been exceeding Clinton in polling match-ups against Trump, in some cases by double digits.

Hillary's campaign was facing a very different but related challenge. She won the party's nomination, but not overwhelmingly: Bernie had taken twenty-two states and won 45 percent of pledged delegates. For Hillary and the Democrats to have a shot in the general election, they would need every one of Bernie's supporters. The Democratic Party Convention, and the events leading up to it, were reserved for building that unity. The Bernie campaign acquiesced, in part because it did not have the votes but also because of the expediency of defeating Donald Trump. What both sides failed to realize, however, was just how committed Bernie's supporters were to the political and social agenda his campaign represented and how deeply entrenched many of them were in movement building outside the electoral domain.

The Democrats also miscalculated the country's general disgust with the political mainstream and the class dynamics that were driving it. Republicans did too. In 2016, voters across the spectrum derided the leadership of both parties as indistinguishable elements of "the establishment." Over the past three to four decades, Democrats and Republicans' shared commitment to US military superiority has been matched by significant crossover in economic priorities, from free trade and financial liberalization to the privatization of public institutions. Such dynamics have made it more and more difficult, if not impossible, for people to forge a decent, middle-class life in this country.

The significance of Bernie's campaign lay in the decisive turn it offered away from policies favoring corporations and the rich, and toward a modern New Deal, marked by universal access to basics like health care and education, re-investment in public institutions, full employment and fair wages, and government regulation to protect workers and the environment. Clinton promised a diverse, prosperous America but in the same breath told poor and middle-class people that their government could not afford basic programs to support them. Her techniques did little to sway young voters, but her wonky, technical arguments did proliferate throughout the corporate media and to this day remain hegemonic in American culture.[1]

The final, official contestation over these divergent political visions and policy agendas took place during the drafting of the party's official platform, before Bernie endorsed Hillary for president on July 12, 2016, and formally conceded the party's nomination at the Democratic National Convention a few weeks later. After such a hotly contested primary, the party's platform was being touted as a kind of peace treaty between Bernie's "political revolution" and the Democratic National Committee (DNC). What establishment Democrats (and Republicans) failed to comprehend, however, was that papering over the rising anti-establishment forces on both Left and Right would only help to crash their party and set the stage for a Donald Trump presidency.

The DNC Platform, Hilton DoubleTree, Orlando, Florida, July 8–9, 2016

The Democrats' national platform had not been a major point of contestation since 1988, when Jesse Jackson offered amendments on military policy, health care, and education and introduced rules to diversify the party. The 1984 convention witnessed four hours of platform discussion, which was nothing compared to the seventeen hours of heated debate in 1980 over Jimmy Carter and Ted Kennedy's fundamental split over unemployment and inflation.[2]

Bill Clinton's platform in 1992 marked a sharp turn from New Deal Democrats' agenda of tax and spend, social safety nets, and full employment, toward one of small government, personal responsibility, and market-driven growth and investment. Subsequent platforms have gone unchallenged, and the convention itself has largely functioned as a political spectacle and coronation. Congressman Barney Frank said as much when he branded the platform the "Miss Congeniality" of the convention process. Frank worked on the 2012 document, but the process was so boring, he intimated, that he couldn't recall what was in it.[3]

Bernie's decision to endorse Hillary and focus on the platform drew ire from some of his movement-based supporters who argued that he should shun Clinton and the Democrats entirely. Why unify with the same party elements that tried to fix the primary process and defame Bernie's character and progressive program? From the perspective of policymaking inside the beltway, however, there was good reason to believe that under a Clinton administration, the political cachet that Bernie accumulated during the primary would have put him at the front of the line for prominent committee assignments. With a seat at the head of the table, he could work with the national constituencies he cultivated during the campaign to fight for a single-payer health care system, free public higher education, improved protections for trade unions, and other progressive policies on the legislative front.

In deciding the platform, the DNC used a faux democratic process. First, a small number of appointees to the DNC Platform Drafting Committee composed an initial draft of the document based on debate and testimony around the country. The document was then ratified by a larger, nationally representative committee, which met in Orlando, Florida, on July 8–9, 2016, to debate amendments. From there, the platform was presented at the party's convention, and any outstanding, contested issue could be submitted to delegates through "minority reports."

While the drafting committee involved sixteen representatives, the larger, national body included 186 platform members. In both cases, the number of appointments was allocated to both presidential candidates based on how they performed in the primaries and caucuses. A similar process was used for appointing representatives to the Rules Committee, which formed a Unity Reform Commission to review the primary and caucus process and superdelegate system and to expand the party.

Bernie's platform representatives were outnumbered by Hillary's, but we did have enough members to bring dissenting minority reports to the convention. The week before the committee met in Orlando, members were instructed to offer amendments to the platform document for vetting by Bernie's campaign staffers. As the representative of Vermont, I collected amendments from local constituents and delegates and received dozens of emails from Vermont advocates for single-payer health care. Staff members processed a gigantic in-flow of amendments and entered more than 200 of them in the official docket. I submitted my own revisions on free public higher education and the platform's appallingly hawkish language on Iran and Palestine, as well as the proposals I'd collected from Vermont constituents.

At the meeting in Orlando, the committee's power to decide the actual contents of the document was largely symbolic. The DNC assembled a few hundred committee members—including members of Congress, trade union presidents, and others—but we basically sat idle for long periods of time while just a handful of unelected staffers from both camps triaged and negotiated amendments in back rooms. One source close to John Podesta told me that the Clinton campaign instructed their staff ahead of time to "just give them what they want. No one will ever remember or care about what's in the platform." Given our side's minority vote status, however, back-door democracy was really the only way to impact the party's agenda moving forward. But one definitely got the impression that the DNC conceived of the process as just for show.

And a show it was. For amendments that the platform committee actually did consider, Hillary's people adopted an organized and covert system for disseminating vote recommendations. Our side was much more transparent, with campaign staffers running feverishly around the hall waving red or green pieces of paper to whip our votes. Vote tallies were displayed at the front of the room on two giant screens that flanked the elevated stage where DNC leadership presided. Between the stage and screens were C-SPAN cameras that swiveled between the DNC chair and the committee.

I described the experience in an essay for the *Nation* as "part NBA final, part Weber's iron cage of bureaucracy," as formal rules of order and predictable vote outcomes were periodically interrupted by grandstanding and uproar from the fired-up gallery in the back of the room. Only on one occasion did the vote tip unexpectedly. Our side proposed an amendment to remove marijuana as a Class 1 drug under the federal Controlled Substances Act. As the ticker inched upward, it became clear that some Clinton representatives had voted for our amendment. When we won, by a margin of a single vote, Bernie staffers jumped up and down on the sidelines, while Hillary supporters scrambled for a revote.

Despite the intended theme of unity, the event had a strong us-versus-them quality. During backroom negotiations, one of Hillary's senior policy advisors, Maya Harris, went on her own personal strike during talks over a $15 minimum wage provision. With the entire room of committee members ready to start voting, she disappeared for several hours and was not available to complete the negotiation. As day passed into night, Bernie's campaign staff and some well-known surrogates rattled cages with higher-ups in the party. We got the $15, but the long delay forced the committee to work late into the morning.

The greatest point of disunity, however, was over trade policy and the Trans-Pacific Partnership (TPP). During the platform drafting committee hearings, Representative Elijah Cummings (the committee chairman) refused to oppose the TPP in the platform because he did "not want to embarrass the president." What we did not know was that Obama had personally called some of Hillary's drafting committee appointees to keep them from formally opposing his signature trade deal.[4]

In Orlando, the press must have anticipated the TPP showdown because C-SPAN's lighting was much brighter that day and its cameras angled perfectly to capture plat-form members' testimony against the official-looking backdrop of the DNC chair. After American Federation of State, County and Municipal Employees (AFSCME) president Lee Saunders delivered his thunderous speech on the perils of "free trade," former National Association for the Advancement of Colored People (NAACP) chief Ben Jealous challenged him in a second order amendment to state his and Clinton's unequivocal opposition to the TPP. Saunders's weak counterpoint was drowned out by murmurs of "shame" and unruly protests from both the floor and the gallery.

I spoke in favor of Jealous's amendment in hopes of appealing to Clinton's female supporters on the basis of how the TPP would especially hurt women. Women com-prise the majority of minimum wage workers in America and would have been affected disproportionately by its downward pressure on wages. It would also have been a death sentence for women with breast and cervical cancer, as exorbitant monopoly pricing was likely to put lifesaving medicines out of reach for many of them.

After Jealous's second order amendment was defeated in the roll call vote, progressive leader Jim Hightower delivered a namesake amendment ("the Hightower Amend-ment") in his classic spitfire language—fingering the TPP as "a little shop of corporate horrors" and offering his amendment as "political Viagra to stiffen the spine of our party." Hightower warned DNC brass that Trump planned to include anti-TPP language in the platform of the GOP. During his testimony, Sanders's representatives defiantly

held up boxes marked anti-TPP to signify the 700,000 sig-
natures the campaign had collected on a petition opposing
the trade deal.

The revisions to the platform that I submitted brought
mixed outcomes. Bernie's proposals for free public higher
education ended up as a "unity amendment" that was negotiated directly between the campaigns prior to the Orlando
meeting. Bernie viewed higher education as a right and
believed that every person in the Unites States deserved a
shot at a college degree, regardless of his or her ability to
pay. Hillary Clinton, and the Democratic Party establishment, conceived of higher education as an industry and as
a commodity. Their negotiation involved setting an eligibility ceiling on free public higher education—a means test
based on income—and, after a few back and forths, they
settled on $125,000, which was projected to cover some 80
percent of the population.

Eighty percent was obviously very good, but the problem
with means tests is that they create unnecessary red tape
for implementers and users alike and offer conservatives an
easy lever for lowering benefits. They also tend to play out
poorly for those whose circumstances put them at the edge
of the threshold, with some people having to quit their jobs
just to qualify for benefits. For people living in high-rent
areas or with other serious financial commitments who can't
afford to lower their incomes in order to qualify, it presents
an unfair catch-22 that can feed into popular resentment
against public programs that have some taxpayers subsidizing the benefits of others. A non-means-tested College for
All avoids all of that and relies on the simple rationale that

America provides free college to all of its people, because the country values higher education as the basis of a good life and as a democratic necessity.

The negotiated language in the final version of the platform document did not end up stipulating a means test, but simply stated that free college should be available to all working families.[5] In light of that ambiguity, I was happy to present Bernie's unity amendment on higher education to the DNC alongside American Federation of Teachers (AFT) president Randi Weingarten.

In addition to free public college, the platform included a long list of items from Sanders's longtime agenda on Wall Street reform—a twenty-first century Glass-Steagall, postal banking, cracking down on the revolving door between Wall Street and Washington, and prohibiting the big banks from choosing which credit agency will rate their products. It also included language on expanding Social Security, banning tax havens, maintaining full employment, and facilitating union membership through majority card-check recognition, in addition to compromises on fracking and renewable energy. The party also committed to abolishing the death penalty, for-profit prisons, and detention centers.

Among the more notable wins in the platform was the party's affirmed commitment to a $15 minimum wage, which Hillary Clinton had not supported during her campaign. Bernie's Herculean efforts in the Senate, as well as grassroots organizing by trade unions, movements like the "Fight for 15," and some state and local governments, have all added up to real progress on raising the minimum wage to a living wage. The $15 wage inscribed in the Democratic Party's platform may or may not become a driving force in the ongoing push for a higher federal minimum wage. But a defeat on the issue certainly could have impeded that work in a significant way. The same could be said of many of the other Bernie "wins" in the platform. Today's Democrats may not be using it as their bible, but the 2016 platform did at least nominally set a baseline policy agenda that is far more progressive than what the party has committed itself to over the last several decades.

At the close of the proceedings, before the meta-vote on the 2016 Democratic Party platform as a whole, Clinton representatives posted a slide on the big screens in the front of the room titled "Unity Amendment." Despite the fact that Bernie had not yet conceded the nomination, the amendment replaced the words "Democratic Nominee" throughout the document with "Hillary Clinton." Bernie supporters went ballistic, with C-SPAN cameras still rolling.

Clinton staffers instantly withdrew the amendment for fear of another public relations calamity. During the uproar, I went over to check in with Cornel West and say goodbye. I knelt next to his chair and watched his eyes narrow as he read the Unity Amendment up on the screen. "They went too far, Sister Heather." He shook his head from side to side, incredulous, "they went toooo far." That was indeed how most of Bernie's supporters and delegates felt heading into the convention—and how many of them still feel today.

The Democratic National Convention, Wells Fargo Center, Philadelphia, July 25–28, 2016

The 2016 Democratic National Convention in Philadelphia lasted four days at the end of July. By the end of Day One, I already felt like I was stuck on a giant cruise ship, chartered by Wells Fargo, Blackstone, and a host of undisclosed others.[6] It was a unique experience, and I was proud to represent the state of Vermont. But like most Bernie delegates, I was totally fed up.

All along, congressional Democrats and corporate media had been taking cheap shots at Bernie's identity and electability and trying to discredit his progressive policy agenda while concealing the elite class program behind theirs. Then, just a few days before the convention, WikiLeaks dropped a bombshell of disclosures that implicated journalists and DNC officials in tipping the scales for Hillary, a project apparently begun much earlier, with Robby Mook trying to rig the primary calendar back in 2014.[7]

On Day One of the convention, I arrived just in time for a scheduled interview with Al Jazeera, fully expecting to discuss the campaign's positions on trade and higher education. Upon entering the press box overlooking the expansive convention floor, however, I was deafened by thunderous anti-Hillary jeering. The reporter queried me about Bernie supporters booing raucously earlier that day when he had expressed support for Clinton against Trump. I confirmed the story to be true: If there was any grassroots-level unity between the campaigns, I hadn't seen it.

The ubiquitous booing continued throughout the

convention, as the DNC rolled out speakers like billionaire Michael Bloomberg and General John Allen—prompting former Republican National Committee chairman Michael Steele to quip on Twitter, "Enjoying this Republican Convention with a 4-Star General commanding the stage and chants of 'USA, USA.'"[8] MSNBC's Joe Scarborough observed something similar—that both Michelle and Barack Obama's speeches proffered "a Reaganesque view of America."[9]

Bernie delegates felt like we were crashing a party for wealthy campaign contributors, lobbyists, and political insiders—and we were.[10] Countless stories circulated during and after the convention of Bernie supporters being threatened and harassed by security guards and DNC staffers, their signs confiscated or purposely obscured by American flags, and some of them kicked out entirely.

The antipathy between us and establishment Democrats showed at the state breakfasts where delegates obtained their daily credentials and socialized with each other and with guest speakers. Our combined Vermont–Maine–New Hampshire breakfast featured a range of political figures, including Robby Mook and Brian Fallon from the Clinton campaign; former Maryland and Vermont governors Martin O'Malley and Howard Dean; and Senators Shaheen, Leahy, Bernie, and others. Each day brought a new round of scuffle among delegates fighting a proxy war for their candidates over single-payer health care and the TPP, and, of course, the content of the WikiLeaks disclosures.

Bernie spoke at our breakfast on Day Three. After the breakfast, I traveled in his motorcade to the Texas delegation, where he appeared with Jim Hightower. New Englanders had our flare-ups, but Texas made headlines for Sanders vs. Clinton delegate infighting. I stood with his staff in the back of the hall, stunned by the senator's enlarged celebrity. Before the election, I could bump into him on Church Street or at the local parade in Vergennes. Now he was mobbed like the Beatles and flanked by Secret Service. The last time I saw him in Middlebury, he was being trailed by a band of giggly little kids.

Some of Bernie's delegates were disappointed in him for having conceded the nomination prior to the convention and endorsing Hillary. Bernie or Busters couldn't bear to vote for her, and some, like West, supported the Greens. Ralph Nader, who'd been critical of the campaign for not running third party, complimented Bernie for his endorsement speech in New Hampshire, saying that he smartly "set her [Hillary] up for political betrayal which will allow him to enlarge his civic mobilization movement after the election."[11]

Congressional Democrats poured salt on the wounds by chastising him for not endorsing right away; when he did come out for her, they complained that his endorsement was too tepid. Beltway pundits claimed that he was burning political capital, and some, like the *Nation*'s Joan Walsh, accused him of tearing the party apart and working to elect Donald Trump.[12] During a speech in the House of Representatives, Democrats went so far as to heckle him for not ceding the nomination quickly enough—which they did, tellingly, just as he asserted that "the goal should not be to win elections," but "to transform America."[13]

Platform committee members, many of them grassroots activists, were also upset with the campaign for failing to submit "minority reports," especially on the issue of the TPP. At the close of the DNC platform meeting in Orlando, members signed reports that, if filed, would have forced a vote at the convention on a handful of amendments, including ones on fracking, Palestine, and the TPP. Given Obama's attachment to the TPP and the Clinton campaign's desperation for shows of unity, such a move would have prolonged the appearance of disunity within the party and potentially cost Bernie valuable political capital.

But for progressive activists outside mainstream politics, especially those with longtime histories of contesting trade liberalization, the convention offered a unique opportunity to throw a national spotlight on the issue of free trade and express dissent directly to the president, the Democratic Party, and an international audience. There was, of course, little chance of getting those amendments on the actual platform, given that we were outnumbered in the delegate vote count. But that did not keep delegates from making a public stand against the TPP at the convention, especially since its main architect, President Obama, was a featured speaker.

In the weeks leading up to the DNC in Philadelphia, my email was lit up with planning for the TPP action and for a large-scale TPP forum on the opening night of the convention. Delegates from Chicago skillfully designed No-TPP signs not detectable in a security screening. We planned to hold them up during Obama's speech on Day Three and chant "No TPP!" Controversy arose, however, over delegates' booing of Congressman Elijah Cummings during his presentation of the party platform. Some delegates and corporate media cried racism because the heckling drowned out Cummings's words on his deceased father and the importance of diversity in the Democratic Party. Recall, however, that it was Cummings who took the lead in blocking anti-TPP language in the party's official platform because he did not want to "embarrass the president"—despite predictions that the job-killing trade deal would most acutely affect people of color and women.[14]

In the email debates beforehand, some delegates argued against protesting Obama because he was the first black president. One self-identified African American woman in the group explained, however, that "Obama has to be held to the same principles we hold everybody else to. It is not racist to interrupt Obama." Another delegate argued,

> My guess is that anyone who would advocate against action on this either does not understand what the TPP does, or they are willing to use identity politics as a shield in order to avoid dealing with the real issues at hand. Just like we are not willing to give Hillary a free pass.

In keeping with the promise to facilitate party unity, the campaign sent out a note from Bernie to his delegates imploring them not to disrupt the convention. Delegates held up the No-TPP signs but were respectful of the president's speech. From my vantage point a few feet away, Bernie and Jane seemed to appreciate the No TPP activism.

I watched the roll call vote on Day Two from the senator's box alongside his top advisors, Phil, David, and

Warren, with one eye on the convention floor and the other on a closed-circuit television at our small bar table. Bernie paced behind us, readying to concede the nomination. His brother, Larry, had just delivered the count for overseas voters, naming their parents, Eli and Dorothy, and remarking sentimentally about how proud they'd be of their son carrying the torch of FDR's New Deal legacy. There wasn't a dry eye in the house.

As the votes came in, Bernie joined us at the table, his eyes glued to the small TV. States that he'd won, some by large margins, came in as ties or losses because of the superdelegates. When Michigan registered "Clinton 76, Sanders 67," Phil rang out, "Hey, we *won* Michigan!" It was the same for Indiana: "Clinton 46, Sanders 44." "We beat her in Indiana!" The worst was New Hampshire, where he not only won by a gaping margin—60 percent to 38 percent—but set the record for the largest number of votes ever. As the tally came in at 16 Bernie, 16 Hillary, the Wells Fargo Center rumbled with applause. Bernie shook his head in disbelief and said soberly, "We won New Hampshire by a *yuge* margin."

My jaw on the floor, I said out loud to no one in particular, "This is SO, so depressing." As the table nodded, Bernie shot me a look through the top rim of his glasses: "Depressing, you say?" I half-smiled, having just uttered the understatement of the century to a man about to concede the party's nomination for president of the United States. He smiled back without an ounce of bitterness, then joined Jane and his Secret Service detail, and was out the door.

Moments later, they appeared on the convention floor amid a proud Vermont delegation. Party chair Dottie Deans delivered an emotional speech about how Bernie "had changed the trajectory of this country in a way that will make lives of working Americans better for generations to come."[15] She then cast Vermont's votes, passed the microphone to him, and he conceded the nomination. Tears flooded my eyes as I strained to read an incoming text from my husband back home in Ferrisburgh: "This country just lost an opportunity."

The General Election and Its Aftermath

The night Democrats lost the White House to Donald Trump lasted about two weeks for many Americans. It was like a bad car accident where the memory of the impact, and the question of its consequence, lingers. Was Trump's America going to be a gold-plated enterprise molded by unadulterated corporate greed? Did his administration plan to institute racist policies like stop-and-frisk and appeal to brazen nationalism by instituting a Muslim registry and deporting DREAMers? Were gay marriages about to be dissolved and abortion clinics forced underground? Would blanket deregulation lead to disastrous oil spills, water contamination, and rabid financial speculation? Was he serious about a nuclear arms race and building a medieval wall that he would force Mexico to pay for?

Republicans who had once spurned Trump began to embrace him. House speaker Paul Ryan giddily pronounced the victory as "the dawn of a new unified Republican government."[16] Ryan hadn't been shy about openly admiring free market utopians like Ayn Rand and the iconic neoclassical economist Friedrich von Hayek.[17] The Clintons may have winked at privatizing entitlements in the past, but for years Ryan had been trying to fully gut America's public institutions and reduce government to nothing more than a police force by and for capital. Now was his big chance.

In 2016, Americans voted in large numbers against establishment elites in both parties. Among the twenty-two states that Bernie won in the nomination process were places hit hard by manufacturing job losses associated with automation and free trade like Michigan and Wisconsin, where Clinton lost to Trump. She also lost by large margins in states with carbon-intensive economies, like Ohio and West Virginia, where environmental regulation is perceived as injurious to the economy. Despite his green agenda, Bernie won those latter two states and polled consistently higher than Clinton against Trump.[18]

One of the great shockers for Clinton and her pundits was that white females, both college-educated and not, voted in unexpectedly large numbers for Donald Trump, even after the release of the *Access Hollywood* tapes and other revelations of his misogyny. The promise of Hillary as the first woman president simply did not register as a win for them. The other major blow was that African American voters did not show up at the polls to compensate for her steep losses among white voters; moreover, a surprising 29 percent of Hispanic voters went for Trump, despite his consistent threats to deport Latin American immigrants and to build a wall.[19]

Critics of the Clinton campaign point to strategic flaws regarding her lack of a ground game in the industrial Midwest and her general plan to build an electoral coalition based on the country's changing demographics and increased minority share of the electorate. Others cite her gaffes and those of other establishment Democrats. (For example, Obama drank from a water bottle in Flint, Michigan, before the system was actually detoxed; Clinton called Trump voters "deplorables" and talked about running West Virginian coal miners out of business.[20]) Moreover, a persistent email scandal fanned the flames of anti-elitism by sharpening her image as living above the law.

Voters' aversion to the Wall Street bailout was an important part of the picture. Trumpism is a response to corporate-led globalization and the financial crisis on a worldwide scale that has pushed elements of mainstream politics to the right, against the enemy of a big government run by liberal elites. As living standards and working conditions for middle-class Americans have steadily decreased, scapegoating narratives have become more and more seductive.

Trump played to those class antagonisms with remarkable acumen. After AFL-CIO president Richard Trumka announced his federation's endorsement for Hillary, Trump declared that the AFL-CIO

> has made clear that it no longer represents American workers … Instead they have become part of the rigged system in Washington, D.C. that benefits only the insiders … I believe their members will be voting for me in much larger numbers than for her.[21]

He wasn't right, but he was uncomfortably close: for decades, union workers have tended to vote for Democrats in presidential elections by margins that hover around 20 percent. In 2016, the difference narrowed to just 8 percent.[22]

Despite the clear writing on the wall, a surprising number of liberal Democrats persisted in putting forth theories of "whitelash" to explain Clinton's loss.[23] Most of those hypotheses failed to address regional variations in political orientation indicated by Obama's electoral popularity in northern industrial states. And they wrongheadedly tried to read complex social and psychological dynamics (racial and gender relations and attitudes) in voting behavior.

While Americans were left with lingering questions regarding the role of racism, sexism, and elitism in shaping the election, much of the resultant discourse continued to treat race and gender politics as detached from class interests, especially the class interests that the Democratic Party establishment continues to represent.

The outcome of the 2016 presidential election will necessarily remain blurred by weak voter turnout, voter suppression, the disparity between the Electoral College and the popular vote, and Trump's lack of popularity within his own party. Regardless of these and other ambiguities, what's clear is that in strategic parts of the country, identity politics failed to legitimize establishment Democrats' elite-driven class program, and it played an important role in undermining the possibility of an authentic progressive turn in US politics that Bernie's campaign represented.

Bernie in Trumpland

In the wake of Trump's election, Democratic Party leadership made a series of moves toward garnering unity between the party establishment and Bernie's progressives. Senate minority leader Chuck Schumer recruited Bernie to a leadership position as outreach chairman. Bernie was the first Independent to undertake a party leadership role since the modern leadership structure was started in the early 1990s. Part of his job involved prompting senators and congressman to mobilize their grassroots bases. He inaugurated those efforts with a nationwide day of rallies against the GOP's plans to repeal Obamacare. Bernie himself appeared in Michigan with Schumer and Michigan senators Debbie Stabenow and Gary Peters and congresswoman Debbie Dingell.

He also promoted new DNC leadership and actively campaigned for congressman Keith Ellison for the post of DNC chair. During that campaign, Ellison expanded the Bernie coalition to include union leaders who had sided with Hillary during the primary, including AFT president Randi Weingarten. Weingarten spoke in favor of Ellison's candidacy at a campaign event at her union's headquarters, broadcast via Livestream to more than one million viewers.[24] Ellison also cultivated support among the new party brass, including Schumer and Senator Elizabeth Warren.

The Obama White House rejected Ellison's candidacy, however, and offered its pro-TPP labor secretary, Tom Perez, as an alternative. Recall that in the lead-up to Nevada, Perez suggested to Clinton that she use identity politics to defame Bernie. The White House used that same play-book to delegitimize Ellison's bid for DNC chair, drawing on 1990s opposition research to paint him as an extremist, referencing sympathetic remarks he'd made about Louis Farrakhan (which Ellison already had retracted). It was a sad replay of the Sanders–Clinton contest, with establishment Democrats once again using identity as a basis for maligning a progressive member of their own party and foregoing the opportunity to at least appear as the party of the poor and middle class.[25] Bernie described the state of affairs with blunt accuracy: "There are some people in the Democratic Party who want to maintain the status quo. They would rather go down with the Titanic so long as they have first-class seats."[26]

Once the results of the race were in, a *New York Times* headline announced, "Democrats Elect Thomas Perez, Establishment Favorite, as Party Chairman." The newly installed President Trump went further on Twitter: "Congratulations to Thomas Perez, who has just been named Chairman of the DNC," he wrote, "I could not be happier for him, or for the Republican Party!"[27]

In late April 2017, Bernie and Perez launched a "Unity Tour," but the headlines remained fixed on the obvious divisions. Bernie still identified as an Independent, despite his higher level of influence in the party; and Perez couldn't coherently answer questions about whether Democrats supported single-payer health care. For leftists and some progressives, the tour looked like an attempt to herd them into the fold of the establishment. For liberals, it looked like pandering to Bernie's base. No one in the leadership apparatus seemed ready to admit that the two men represented fundamentally divergent class interests: One side sought to elevate the public sector in the service of the working class; the other side promoted free trade and public–private partnerships that privileged corporate interests.

In mid-December, Bernie took part in a televised town hall meeting sponsored by MSNBC's *All In With Chris Hayes* at the United Automobile Workers Local 72 in Kenosha County, Wisconsin—a state that Hillary famously skipped while campaigning against Trump. The event was called "Bernie Sanders in Trump Country," which wasn't quite accurate: Kenosha hadn't voted for a Republican in a presidential election in nearly a half a century, and Trump won the county by just a slim margin of fewer than 300 votes. The concept, however, was spot-on: Bernie was there to connect with former Democratic voters and to understand why they broke for Trump in 2016.[28]

When asked, the Trump voters who participated in the event distanced themselves from their candidate's xenophobia and explained away his campaign promises to deport Mexicans and ban Muslims as idle threats. Congress and the Supreme Court, they said, would never let that happen. One of them, who said he had planned to vote for Bernie, remarked that he voted for Trump "basically, because he wasn't Hillary." A Republican union member expounded that in Kenosha, and other parts of the state, voters preferred either Bernie and Trump, but none of the others, and especially not Clinton.

Yet even with Bernie, some beefed: Who was going to

pay for universal free college and health care? Wouldn't raising the minimum wage also raise prices? One woman admitted that she *did* hope that Trump would deport the "illegals" at her factory because, she said, they were driving down her wages and cheating the tax system.

She also brought up funding for Medicare, Medicaid, and Social Security. In what seemed like a direct message to the GOP, Bernie asked her if she believed that those programs should be cut. "No," she answered firmly. He then pointed to the massive "trillions of dollars" transfer of wealth "from you to the 1 percent" that had transpired over the last three to four decades and asked: "Do you think it's inappropriate to ask those people to start paying their fair share of taxes, so we can adequately fund Medicaid and making public colleges and universities tuition free?" "They got rich off us," she responded, "So it's time they put back." On that, they could all agree.

Despite the Clintons' political history, and Hillary's disconnect with working-class people in 2016, liberals tried to characterize outreach to Trump voters as pandering to racists and sexists. Did they think that the Democratic Party should simply abandon the tens of millions of Americans who voted for Trump for an unknowable complex of reasons—which included "Please God, anyone but her"? Should Democratic presidential candidates just skip Wisconsin and belittle poor whites at Manhattan fund-raisers? Should we just let off the hook the multinational corporations and corrupt politicians who've ruined whole parts of the country—by retrenching on public schools, spoiling the air and water in poor regions, flatlining the minimum wage, brokering job-killing trade deals, and allowing Big Pharma to peddle opioids to vulnerable people? Why weren't liberals questioning the Democrats' role in exacerbating such trends, and their part in enabling a Trump presidency?

One of the more instructive moments for understanding Bernie's distinction from Democratic Party liberals occurred during the campaign when he spoke at Liberty University. Liberty was founded by late televangelist preacher Jerry Falwell and is one of the country's most conservative institutions of higher education. When I asked Bernie's communications guru, Michael Briggs, about the decision to appear there, he explained that the campaign received a stock invitation sent to all 2016 presidential candidates, and, quite simply, they accepted it. The last Democrat to speak at Liberty was Ted Kennedy, and that was three decades ago.[29]

Similar to speeches he had delivered to conservative audiences in Vermont, Bernie began his speech by acknowledging differences between his outlook and what he suspected to be those of Liberty's faculty and students: He declared his support for gay marriage, a woman's right to choose, and the fight against climate change. He then spent the remainder (the majority) of his talk discussing what progressives and conservatives have in common. He quoted scripture, referenced the golden rule, and cited Pope Francis's profound ethical statements against economic inequality—"Money must serve, not rule." And he appealed to the students' sense of morality regarding a system in which "so few have so much, and so many have so little." Briggs said that during their lunch, Falwell, Jr., expressed gratitude to Bernie for his visit and delight that the students responded so positively, given how liberals tend to stonewall conservatives at US universities.

The theme of 2016 was the indictment of party elites on both sides of the aisle, who had more in common with each other than they did with their own respective bases. The emerging electoral power of anti-elite forces in the United States was in part foreshadowed by the ousting of House majority leader Eric Cantor during the Virginia primary in 2014 by obscure Tea Party professor David Brat. Brat's low-budget campaign framed Cantor as out of touch with his base and in cahoots with rich businessmen like Mark Zuckerberg to outsource American jobs.[30] By playing the class card with populist fervor, and playing to the reactionary passions and insecurities of a recession-battered people, he unseated a seven-term incumbent next in line for speaker of the house. Donald Trump seized that baton in 2016, and he ran with it.

Bernie's populism was rooted in a profoundly different kind of anti-elitism that drew masses of young people in search of a more tolerant and egalitarian future, against the jobless, debt-ridden one that the Clinton–Wall Street alliance offered. Despite early and glaring warning signs, Clinton's campaign remained remarkably blind to the political reality that class anxieties and anti-liberalism were imbuing the mood of the election, as was a yearning, especially among young people, for a trustworthy and charismatic savior.

Hillary won the popular vote by almost 3 million votes. But she did not win the race.[31] Her campaign cited a diversity of culprits—from Bernie to James Comey to Vladimir Putin—as well as racism and misogyny among white Trump voters. Comey's eleventh-hour intervention *did* help tank her in the polls. And the Russian hacks and email leaks *did* paint a sordid picture of a conniving political team so obsessed with winning they'd exploit the tragedies of Sandy Hook—and so tone-deaf to the class war around them, they'd scheme to help Trump win the nomination because they thought he'd be easier to beat.[32]

But what's important to consider for the sake of moving forward is that, like Clinton's neoliberalism, Trumpism does not offer a viable framework for unifying various segments of the population. Nor does it offer a means for addressing the higher education crisis, the sending of US jobs offshore, permanent war and climate change, widespread economic insecurity, and the lack of affordable health care. Trump may have put liberals, progressives, and the Left on the defensive, but he also left a gaping hole for a more diverse and class-conscious political movement to emerge and to offer real solutions to the most pressing issues of our time.

Conclusion:
Campaigns End,
Movements Endure

This book is one of what should be many aimed at processing the contradictions and lessons learned from Bernie's campaign and the presidential election more generally. The year 2016 may have signaled a crashing of the Democratic establishment, but it also opened a door for the party to reconstitute itself, forge new political alliances, and build a new relationship with working-class people—while revising its frameworks of racial and gender equality, sexual freedom, and clean environment.

Lessons Learned

1. Problems of Social Inequality Require Structural Solutions

One critical lesson of 2016 regards the question of how to build movements and political organizations capable of confronting persistent problems of race, gender, and class inequality in America. Neoliberals on the side of Clinton patently rejected the idea that racial and gender-based injustice could be alleviated through universal forms of public investment. Instead they offered individual inclusion and mobility in consumer society as a solution—and let capital off the hook.

If Democrats are genuinely interested in mitigating racial and gender disparities in the country, they will have to start considering these disparities in terms of the structural dynamics of the larger political economy. That means implicating the fundamentals of contemporary capitalism—profit motives, global finance, and ruling class power—and the racial and gender ideologies that help legitimize them.

Hillary's delinking of race and gender from class-based inequality was apparent in her campaign's "New America" strategy—which involved building an electoral coalition based on changing demographics and an increasing minority share of the electorate that also included Wall Street bankers, Silicon Valley elites, and a racially diverse professional managerial class. She wooed wealthier centrist Republicans, while openly insulting working people and their advocates with terms like "flyover states" and "deplorables." She did little to court voters in the industrial Midwest and Appalachia and, when discussing clean energy in West Virginia, declared, "We're going to put a lot of coal miners and coal companies out of business."[1]

Despite her status as one of history's most elite politicians, living in the rich white suburb of Chappaqua, New York, Clinton advertised herself as the race- and gender-conscious "first woman" candidate. Such "diversity" branding has become one of the more potent tools of elites to render their interests universal, while obscuring the reality of a system stacked in their favor. When treated as its own end, diversity can create appearances of progressiveness and enlightenment (especially next to troglodytes like Trump) that both distract from, and even sell, policies that hurt poor and working-class people. That's at least partly why Hillary's appeals to feminism fell flat among white women and why so many black and Hispanic voters did not show up to the polls, voter suppression notwithstanding.[2]

Analyses of Trump's victory will necessarily remain blurred by weak voter turnout and the disparity between the Electoral College and the popular vote. But what's clear from 2016 is that establishment Democrats failed to address the material needs and aspirations of poor and working-class Americans of all backgrounds that have been structurally subordinated to the material interests of the ruling class.

2. Building a Mass Constituency for Left or Progressive Policies Requires Grassroots Organizing

A second lesson regards the increasing centrality of social media in electoral and movement politics, which, for the latter, stems from the organizational and publicity successes of the Arab Spring, Occupy Wall Street, and Black Lives Matter—and before that, the alter-globalization movement and Zapatistas, who were among the first to use the Internet to globalize their struggle.[3] Platforms like Facebook and Twitter have become potent outreach and organizing tools, and they enable decentralized "self-organization," which has become the new way of doing insurgent politics.

It is important to note, however, that in the Egyptian manifestation of the Arab Spring, the Mubarak government was brought down by gigantic numbers of protestors physically assembled in Tahrir Square, in addition to pressure by the military and other state power players.[4] Tunisians' defeat of President Zine El Abidine Ben Ali was largely advanced by trade unions in solidarity with other movement actors, as were the protests in Wisconsin against Scott Walker and Occupy Wall Street a few months later.[5] To paint those formations as self-organized and catalyzed through social media is to underestimate the importance of face-to-face assembly and the vital resources that formal institutions—like unions, NGOs, universities, and some state actors—bring to the table and their capacities for massive, on-the-ground organizing.

Social media has enabled left-leaning intellectuals and activists, as well as high-profile presidential candidates like Bernie, and Trump, to proliferate discourses on issues that corporate media is not inclined to cover. And it can help staffers from all kinds of political institutions perform the work of outreach with remarkable speed. Bernie's expansive online presence and spectacular rallies undeniably raised his own personal popularity and that of his agenda, which was critical, given his low name recognition early on. Among the risks of too much emphasis on online organizing, however, is that it can easily unhinge from actual struggles and reduce political engagement to hashtags and slogans.

It can also create the appearance of social forces that don't actually exist. A study conducted by two University of Southern California researchers found that some 20 percent of Twitter traffic on the 2016 election was conducted by bots, many of which spread misinformation and vitriolic, partisan messaging.[6] Movements like Occupy Wall Street, moreover, may have involved hundreds of local Occupys, but some of them consisted of just a few dudes in a high school computer lab. Same for the local social forums associated with the World Social Forum—the anti–World Economic Forum born in Porto Alegre, Brazil, that spawned hundreds of local and regional social forums around the world.[7] Many of those local forums attracted significant numbers from their communities, but others maintained an online presence long after their numbers dwindled.

In a general election postmortem, labor expert Kim Moody signaled the very un-progressive political economic dynamics underlying today's electoral campaigns' increasing reliance on social media and television advertising, pointing out that

> working-class voter participation has remained low in part because the political parties have reduced the direct door-to-door human contact with lower-income voters in favor of purchased forms of campaigning, from TV ads to the new digitized methods of targeting likely voters.[8]

Moody describes how private companies accumulate large databases of voters' personal information and sell that data to electoral campaigns. Candidates use the information to target specific groups on social media platforms like Facebook, which apparently made hundreds of millions of dollars in 2016 through digital ad buys.[9]

3. Electoral Campaigns and Social Movements Are Not the Same Thing

A third lesson regards the relationship between electoral campaigns and social movements. Much ink was spilled in the immediate aftermath of the primary speculating on what Bernie's armies of volunteers, small donors, and Twitter followers would do next—in other words, where all that progressive grassroots energy would go, especially as Bernie turned his attention to the Democratic Party platform and to campaigning against Donald Trump.

Even if Bernie had won the presidency, his incredible popularity was not likely to translate into immediate policy wins without a major expansion of his popular base. The Right and those in corporate power (including some Democrats) would have come at him like a freight train, and too much of the electorate still believes that universal programs like single-payer health care and college for all are not fair or viable—though that is changing. A constituency powerful and sustainable enough to fuel the kind of political agenda that Bernie proposed—to redistribute wealth and political power to poor and working-class people—has yet to be made.

Bernie's campaign was unlike most in that its goal was to ignite the grassroots. Normally it works the other way around, with candidates representing the will of an already formed movement, like when the anti-apartheid struggle culminated in Nelson Mandela becoming president of South Africa, the Cochabamba protests ushered Evo Morales's presidency, and the Tea Party infiltrated the GOP.

The good news of 2016 is that a mass constituency does exist for programs to revitalize the public sector, protect the environment, and stem mass incarceration and other forms of state violence; and that large numbers of people across the political spectrum want to get big money out of politics and move beyond the United States' Super Bowl style of electioneering. The bad news is that a seemingly significant constituency also exists for Trump's brand of neo-fascist politics—involving forms of racial and gender hatred not reducible to class antagonisms and economic disenfranchisement.

Although Bernie's campaign engaged in a great deal of on-the-ground organizing, it may have missed an opportunity to engage in more systematic movement-building activities. Part of that is due to the fact that electoral enterprises necessarily operate according to different sets of principles and imperatives than do movements. It is the job of political consultants and staffers to concern themselves with optics, staging, and their own "punch lists," rather than constructing lasting democratic organizations and grassroots networks. They think in terms of candidates and events, rather than collectives and organizational dynamics of social and political change.

Especially after Iowa and New Hampshire, where Bernie did phenomenally well, the campaign put much of its resources into what most campaigns set out to do: win the election. That meant creating spectacular, stadium-size events, prioritizing TV ads, celebrity surrogates, fund-raising, negotiating party rules and structures—as well as targeting constituencies based on abstractions of real people into advertising categories like "millennials" and "the woman vote." Left and progressive movements tend to eschew those kinds of objectifications, however. In fact, increasing numbers of them identify as "leaderless" to signal their rejection of top-down organizing and cults of personality.

Social movements are organic forms of expression, not bound by the same temporal, political, and institutional horizons as electoral campaigns. They tend to coalesce around material interests that shape ideas about social change and, if effective, find ways to operationalize those ideas into short- and long-term goals and realize those goals through contestation and organization.

Electoral campaigns can be part of that calculus, but meaningful change doesn't happen over an election cycle. Conspicuous politics, like conspicuous consumption, plays well on Facebook with "friends" and "likes," but building coalitions and broad bases of support involves deeper forms of organizing than what stadium rallies and Twitter can garner. Americans like to score their history with the thunder of populist prophets and revolutionary heroes, but confronting entrenched power requires much more than popularity contests and mononyms like Hillary and Bernie.

One way that future progressive electoral campaigns could improve upon the movement-building aspects of

Bernie 2016 would be to invest larger sums in field organizing and building local political organizations—comparable to the resources they spend on TV ads, consultants, and digital media. Groups like Labor for Bernie, People for Bernie, Higher Ed for Bernie, and many others did some of that groundwork during the campaign, and Our Revolution took on that role afterwards, and remains active. Left and progressive campaigns could also take a lesson from the Right and encourage deeper engagement in "the war of ideas"—building left-leaning think tanks, academic institutes, book publishers, magazines, and journals—instead of focusing on the horse race aspect of elections and privileging celebrity over collectivity.

Our Revolution

Our Revolution, the successor to the Bernie campaign, is attempting to bridge the movement–electoral divide by rooting local and state electoral campaigns in movement organizations and advocacy groups. Our Revolution was founded in August 2016 and is supported by a staff and board of directors largely comprised of organizers and volunteers from Bernie's campaign. It was established as a 501(c)(4)—a social welfare organization—with the mission to "transform American politics to make our political and economic systems once again responsive to the needs of working families."

The Sanders Institute was also announced in August 2016, and its activities launched around the time of this writing. The institute was founded by Jane Sanders as a nonprofit educational organization "dedicated to transforming our democracy through research, education, outreach and advancement of bold, progressive ideas and values."

Our Revolution set out to advance Bernie 2016's policy agenda—universal higher education, health care, climate change, jobs and infrastructure, free trade—and to build a constituency for it in and outside the Democratic Party. The organization is evolving toward a bottom-up model, in which local groups organize chapters and some coalesce into statewide organizations. Currently, Our Revolution involves roughly 500 registered groups and has strongholds in four states—Maryland, Massachusetts, Wisconsin, and Texas—with several other statewide efforts on tap.

As a collective, Our Revolution's hundreds of groups are involved in activities at the local, state, and national levels, organized around key issue areas ranging from local rent control to debt-free college and Medicare for All. That activity manifests in a variety of forms, including electoral campaigns and ballot measures, campus organizing, and protest and resistance. The group participated in street demonstrations in support of sanctuary cities, for instance, and was active in the airport actions against Trump's Muslim ban. Our Revolution also promotes issue campaigns; during the lame duck session of Congress in 2016, for example, activists made tens of thousands of calls to members of Congress to stop the passing of the Trans-Pacific Partnership.

In addition, Our Revolution engages in local party building and running progressive candidates, from seats on education boards and state senates to gubernatorial and mayoral races. In November 2017, candidates across the country who were endorsed by Our Revolution won seats in local and statewide races and ballot initiatives. Notable among them was Randall Woodfin, who became mayor of Birmingham, Alabama, by defeating incumbent William Bell with the support of dozens of Our Revolution volunteers. In Maine, the organization organized around, and helped win, a ballot measure to implement the first statewide Medicaid expansion.

On matters of class, racial, and gender inequality, Our Revolution president Nina Turner discussed her vision in an interview with the *Nation*. She spoke about forging partnerships with groups that have a sole focus on people of color, while maintaining a class-conscious view of social change: "Working class is working class, whether you're black or white or Hispanic or Asian or Native American. If you're poor, you're poor."[10] Turner identified attempts by ruling class elites to "drive wedges between working-class whites and working-class blacks and Hispanics and other people of color" as an age-old "divide and conquer" tactic.

> I don't want our white working class sisters and brothers to feel as though their pain is not important because it is … But at the same time, I want my white sisters and brothers to understand that when we talk about income and wealth inequality, that disproportionately African Americans suffer a little more. That's an honest conversation.[11]

In terms of how Our Revolution relates to the Democratic Party, the organization's overall goal is to transform and enlarge it and to root it in the needs of working people—their jobs, rights, health care, education, housing, and other aspects of their everyday existence. The group has a Labor for Our Revolution arm, but similar to the campaign, there's a tension between the transactional nature of labor union politics and the aspirational aspect of movement building.

Our Revolution wants to engage working-class people in electoral leadership, but its larger goal extends beyond winning elections. Like the Tea Party, its politics are driven by conviction, values, and desires for social change. Unlike the Tea Party's relationship to the GOP, however, Our Revolution doesn't want to crash the Democratic Party and foment chaos, it wants to rebuild it and expand its reach. In that vein, it's trying to create a home for the masses of activists and voters who were alienated from the Democratic Party establishment before and during 2016—some of whom still identify as Democrats, and others who are agnostic but interested in progressive and left organizing.

Moving Forward

Trump's America is a world of nihilism and flux. His ascendancy summoned reactionary elements from out of the shadows, brought a terrifying surge in hate crimes, and has made life a living hell for millions of immigrants. His shadiness and megalomania are disordering the news media, and his aggrandizement of right-wing propagandists has chilled free speech. The Trump family's footsying with the Putin government and brazen conflicts of interest have elevated corruption to the status of given. At the quotidian level, workplaces have become more irritable and debates at the dinner table more acerbic. Americans who felt insulted by the chicaneries of their neoliberal government are now having to confront the more brutal realities of neo-fascism.

In the months immediately following the election, various groups and movements—both left and liberal, Pantsuit Nation and Berniecrat—took to the streets to challenge the new president's legitimacy. They worked to obstruct his reactionary policy agenda and to hold both Republicans and Democrats accountable, especially during confirmation hearings of cabinet members like Attorney General Jeff Sessions and Education Secretary Betsy DeVos. The Women's March drew tens of millions around the country to defend women's rights against Trump's and others' misogyny. The violent and sudden execution of Trump's Muslim ban drew pointed contestations at airports around the country, which lent a popular element to the heroic legal battles undertaken by the American Civil Liberties Union and some state attorneys general. Republican congressmen's attempts to repeal and replace Obamacare, which would have dropped tens of millions of Americans off their health insurance, were met with heated resistance—at town hall meetings and record-breaking volumes of constituent calls to senators and members of Congress—that decisively helped to thwart the legislation.

The majority of Senate Democrats responded to the new climate by banding together over cabinet confirmations and through legislative appeals to Bernie's progressive base. Forty-five of the forty-eight Senate Democrats led by

Chuck Schumer signed a letter of principles addressed to GOP leadership asking that tax reform not increase the burden on the middle class; not benefit the wealthiest Americans; and not involve cutting Medicare, Medicaid, and Social Security.[12] In addition, a surprising number of co-sponsors—sixteen in all—signed on to Bernie's Medicare for All bill, many of them 2020 presidential hopefuls including senators Elizabeth Warren, Corey Booker, and Kamala Harris. Increased public support in national polls for a single-payer health care program likely attracted some of them to the cause, but the more controversial aspect of how to pay for universal health care—its redistributive aspect—remains an open question for Democrats.

During the Democratic Party primary in 2016, a clear line was drawn in the sand between the pro-Walmart, pro–Wall Street, means-test-loving candidate on one side and, on the other, a pro-worker, anti-austerity candidate, who wanted to redistribute the wealth of the billionaire class. A vast majority of US senators and members of Congress chose the wrong side of history, and now the country is paying a steep price. At the time of this writing, some of those now penitent elected officials, along with the Democratic National Committee and the party's outer layer—of think tanks, donors, for-profit tech companies, and consultants—are recalibrating themselves to the Trump presidency and the growing Left and progressive forces it has unleashed. Because of those forces, there is no doubt that in 2020, if not before, the line between politicians paying lip service to social justice versus those willing to fight for a truly egalitarian distribution of wealth in America will once again shape the outcome of the election.

Whether Bernie himself will enter the race is unsure, but his impact will be unmistakable. As he himself said on the shores of Lake Champlain, the success of his 2016 presidential campaign, and his ongoing, widespread popularity should not be understood as a victory for any single politician, political party, or faction. It should be viewed, rather, as a victory for the idea that public goods and institutions are a necessary part of a just and fair society. Fighting for the survival and de-commodification of those institutions should top Americans' agenda moving forward, regardless of party and identity, and could serve as a basis for the further coming together of diverse communities, movements, and organizations to make a better world.

Notes

Foreword

1. Luke Savage, in a very perceptive essay ("How Liberals Fell in Love with *The West Wing*," *Current Affairs,* April 16, 2017) links the mindset behind that Clintonite approach to consolidation of a Democratic liberalism that values process over substantive political goals and performance of competence over inspiring vision and actively disdains explicit ideological commitment: "Despite its relatively thin ideological commitments, there is a general tenor to the West Wing universe that cannot be called anything other than smug. It's a smugness born of the view that politics is less a terrain of clashing values and interests than a perpetual pitting of the clever against the ignorant and obtuse. The clever wield facts and reason, while the foolish cling to effortlessly exposed fictions and the braying prejudices of provincial rubes. In emphasizing intelligence over ideology, what follows is a fetishization of 'elevated discourse' regardless of its actual outcomes or conclusions. The greatest political victories involve semantically dismantling an opponent's argument or exposing its hypocrisy,

usually by way of some grand rhetorical gesture. Categories like left and right become less significant, provided that the competing interlocutors are deemed respectably smart and practice the designated etiquette. The Discourse becomes a category of its own, to be protected and nourished by Serious People conversing respectfully while shutting down the stupid with heavy-handed moral sanctimony." He summarizes it succinctly as a "Democratic politics increasingly incubated in the Ivy League rather than the labor movement."

2. Jane McAlevey, *No Shortcuts: Organizing for Power in the New Gilded Age*, New York and Oxford: Oxford University Press, 2016, makes a clear, powerful argument for the significance of the distinction between organizing and mobilizing and the paramount importance, especially in the current political situation, of the former.

3. Michael Zweig, *The Working Class Majority: America's Best Kept Secret*, Ithaca: Cornell University Press, 2011.

4. For discussion of the Labor Party effort, its premises, composition, and approach, see Mark Dudzic and Katherine Isaac, "Labor Party Time? Not Yet," thelaborparty.org, December 2012; Derek Seidman, "Looking Back at the Labor Party: An Interview with Mark Dudzic," *New Labor Forum* 23, Winter 2014, pp. 60–64; Adolph Reed, Jr., "Response to Labor Party Interview," *New Labor Forum* 23, Winter 2014, pp. 65–67; and Mark Dudzic and Adolph Reed, Jr., "The Crisis of Labour and the Left in the United States," *Socialist Register*, 2015, pp. 351–75.

5. Adolph Reed, Jr., "Mazzocchi and the Moment," nonsite.org, November 21, 2016.

6. For anecdotal illustrations of this possibility, see Leslie Lopez, "'I Believe Trump Like I Believed Obama!' A Case Study of Two Working-Class 'Latino' Voters: My Parents," nonsite.org, November 28, 2016, and Christian Parenti, "Listening to Trump," nonsite.org, November 17, 2016. Among those neoliberal leftists

who insist that white working-class support of Trump reduces to racism, a main response to the phenomenon of white working-class voters who supported Obama in 2008 and/or 2012 and then Trump in 2016 has been to assert that voting for Obama did not mean that one is not a racist. Of course, they fail to acknowledge the reciprocal point that voting for Trump, therefore, does not mean that one necessarily *is* one.

7. Mark Dudzic, "The Origin of the Species," nonsite.org, January 25, 2017. Regarding the "damage" to Clinton by her association with Obama, see Joan Walsh, "What's Wrong with Bernie Sanders's Strategy," *Nation*, March 21, 2016. On the racial and gender composition of the working class, see Valerie Wilson, "People of Color Will Be a Majority of the American Working Class in 2032," *Economic Policy Institute*, June 9, 2016.

Introduction

1. Philip Bump, "The Decimation of the Democratic Party, Visualized," *Washington Post*, November 10, 2016. See also Bernie Sanders, "Bernie Sanders: How Democrats Can Stop Losing Elections," *New York Times*, June 13, 2017.

2. US House of Representatives, "Party Divisions of the House of Representatives," *History, Art and Archives: US House of Representatives*, history.house.gov. See also US Senate, "Senate History: Party Divisions," senate.gov; and Stephen Wolf, "Republicans Now Dominate State Government, with 32 Legislatures and 33 Governors," *Daily Kos*, November 14, 2016.

3. Kevin Phillips, *Wealth and Democracy: A Political History of the American Rich*, New York: Broadway Books, 2002, p. 92. See also Peter Dreier, "Reagan's Legacy: Homelessness in America," *Shelterforce online*, Issue #135, May/June 2004; Edward A. Gargan, "City Welfare Rolls Climbing Again, Over 900,000," *New York Times*, December 17, 1983; and David Harvey, *A Brief*

History of Neoliberalism, Cambridge: Oxford University Press, 2007, p. 25.

4. President Ronald Reagan, "The President's News Conference," The American Presidency Project, University of California, Santa Barbara, June 28, 1983. See also Bernie Sanders (with Huck Gutman), *Outsider in the House*, New York: Verso, 1988.

5. Knight-Ridder Newspapers, "Social Security Cuts from Reagan Years Being Restored," *Chicago Tribune*, December 4, 1989. See also Robert Pear, "New Reagan Policy to Cut Benefits for the Aged, Blind and Disabled," *New York Times*, October 16, 1987.

6. Rachel Black and Aleta Sprague, "The 'Welfare Queen' Is a Lie," *Atlantic*, September 28, 2016.

7. Heather Gautney, "Taking American Leadership Back from Political Elites," *Washington Post*, June 18, 2014.

1. Crashing the Party

1. Thomas Piketty, "Thomas Piketty on the Rise of Bernie Sanders: The US Enters a New Political Era," *Guardian*, February 16, 2016.

2. Eric Foner, "How Bernie Sanders Should Talk About Democratic Socialism," *Nation*, October 21, 2015.

3. Bernie Sanders, "Bernie Sanders: My Vision for Democratic Socialism in America," *In These Times*, November 19, 2015.

4. Foner, "How Bernie Sanders Should Talk About Democratic Socialism." Quotes in the paragraph are taken from this text.

5. George Souvlis and Cornel West, "Black America's Neoliberal Sleepwalking Is Coming to an End," *OpenDemocracy*, June 13, 2016.

6. "Bernie Sanders vs. Alan Greenspan," Youtube.com, published May 17, 2015.

7. Bernie Sanders, "What Do the Koch Brothers Want?" Bernie Sanders Senate Office (homepage), December 13, 2017.

8. Judith Stein, *Pivotal Decade: How the United States Traded*

Factories for Finance in the Seventies, New Haven: Yale University Press, 2011.

9. For a comprehensive analysis of these historical developments, and those covered in the upcoming paragraphs, see Leo Panitch and Sam Gindin, *The Making of American Capitalism: The Political Economy of American Empire*, London: Verso, 2012. See also Dennis Judd, "Symbolic Politics and Urban Politics: Why African Americans Got So Little from the Democrats," in *Without Justice for All*, ed. Adolph Reed, Jr., Boulder, CO: Westview Press, 1999, pp. 126–31.

10. Gordon Lafer, *The Job Training Charade*, Ithaca, NY: Cornell University Press, 2002, p. 180.

11. Jimmy Carter, "Anti-Inflation Program Address to the Nation," The American Presidency Project, University of California, Santa Barbara, October 24, 1978.

12. Jimmy Carter, "Airline Deregulation Act of 1978 Remarks on Signing S. 2493 into Law," The American Presidency Project, University of California, Santa Barbara, October 24, 1978. See also Panitch and Gindin, *The Making of American Capitalism*, p. 166; and Paul Stephen Dempsey, "Airline Deregulation and Laissez-Faire Mythology: Economic Theory in Turbulence," *Journal of Air Law and Commerce* 56, 1990.

13. Matthew Sherman, "Report: A Short History of Financial Deregulation in the United States," *Center for Economic and Policy Research*, July 20, 2009.

14. Kevin Phillips, *Wealth and Democracy: A Political History of the American Rich*, New York: Broadway Books, 2002, pp. 88–93.

15. Dudzic and Reed, Jr., "The Crisis of Labour and the Left in the United States."

16. Larry Cohen, "We Believe that We Can Win!" *New Labor Forum* 26: 1, 2017, pp. 10–17.

17. Pierre Bourdieu, "The Essence of Neoliberalism," *Le Monde Diplomatique*, December 1998.

18. Peter T. Kilborn, "Democrats Search for a Winning Issue," *New York Times*, February 26, 1984. See also Democratic Party Platform Standing Committee, "Renewing America's Promise: A Report from the Platform Committee," The American Presidency Project, University of California, Santa Barbara, August 13, 2008.

19. Bernard Weinraub, "Mondale Seeks $175 Billion Cut in 1989 Deficit," *New York Times*, September 10, 1984.

20. Eric Laursen, *The Peoples Pension: The Struggle to Defend Social Security Since Reagan*, Oakland: AK Press, 2012, p. 198.

21. William Safire, "Essay: Perot Versus Social Security," *New York Times*, June 15, 1992.

22. William J. Clinton, "Address Accepting the Presidential Nomination at the Democratic National Convention in New York," The American Presidency Project, University of California, Santa Barbara, July 16, 1992.

23. Peter G. Peterson, *The Education of an American Dreamer: How a Son of Greek Immigrants Learned His Way from a Nebraska Diner to Washington, Wall Street, and Beyond*, New York: Twelve, 2009.

24. Robert Pear, "Attacks Begin on Plan to Cut Social Programs," *New York Times*, December 10, 1994.

25. Martin Feldstein, "Social Security Reform and Fiscal Policy in the Clinton Administration," National Bureau of Economic Research (website). Remarks presented at the Harvard University conference on Economic Policy in the 1990s, June 28, 2001. See also Dean Baker, "Bill Clinton, Who's Known for His Plan to Cut Social Security," *Center for Economic and Policy Research* (blog), May 26, 2011.

26. Katha Pollitt, "The Strange Death of Liberal America," *Nation*, August 26–September 2, 1996.

27. "1996 Democratic Party Platform," The American Presidency Project, University of California, Santa Barbara, August 26, 1996.

28. Ned Resnikoff, "The Other Party of Thatcher: The Democrats and New Labour," *NBC News*, April 9, 2013.

29. Ife Lloyd, LaDonna Pavetti, and Liz Schott, "TANF Reaching Few Poor Families," Center for Budget and Policy Priorities, March 30, 2017.

30. Doug Henwood, *My Turn: Hillary Clinton Targets the Presidency*, New York: OR Books, 2015. See also Michelle Alexander, "Why Hillary Clinton Doesn't Deserve the Black Vote," *Nation*, February 10, 2016.

31. Alexander, "Why Hillary Clinton Doesn't Deserve the Black Vote."

32. Leo Panitch and Sam Ginden, *The Making of Global Capitalism: The Political Economy of American Empire*, New York: Verso, 2013. See also Doug Henwood, *After the New Economy: The Binge … and the Hangover That Won't Go Away*, New York: The New Press, 2003.

33. Heather Gautney and Akim Reinhardt, "The Imperial Coin," *Peace and Change* 35: 1, January 2010, pp. 146–63.

34. Adolph Reed, Jr., "Obama No," *Progressive*, April 28, 2008. See also Julie Bosman, "Obama Sharply Assails Absent Black Fathers," *New York Times*, June 16, 2008.

35. Jane Mayer, *Dark Money: The Hidden History of Billionaires Behind the Rise of Radical Right*, New York: Doubleday, 2016, p. 9.

36. Jeff Zeleny, "The President Is on the Line to Follow Up on Socialism," *New York Times*, March 8, 2009.

37. Heather Gautney, "Why the Trans-Pacific Partnership Is Bad for Workers, and for Democracy," *Huffington Post*, February 3, 2015.

38. Mike Snyder, "Americans Families Finally Got a Big Pay Raise. Why It Might Not Feel Like It," *USA Today*, September 13, 2016. See also Mishel Lawrence, Josh Bivens, Elise Gould, and Heidi Shierholz, *The State of Working America, 12th Edition*, Ithaca, NY: Cornell University Press, 2012.

39. Michael Kruse and Manu Raju, "Can Bernie Sanders Win the Love of a Party He Scorns?," *Politico*, August 10, 2015.

40. Paul Starr, "Bernie Sanders's Problem with Democrats," *Atlantic*, February 8, 2016.

41. Kruse and Raju, "Can Bernie Sanders Win the Love of a Party He Scorns?"

42. Nomi Prins, *All the President's Bankers: The Hidden Alliances That Drive American Power*, New York: Nation Books, 2014, pp. 334–41.

43. Leo Panitch and Sam Ginden, *The Making of Global Capitalism: The Political Economy of American Empire*, New York: Verso, 2013, pp. 173–74.

44. The six biggest banks control more than 95 percent of derivatives, 40 percent of bank deposits, and more than 66 percent of all credit cards. Bernie Sanders, *Our Revolution: A Future to Believe In*, New York: Thomas Dunne Books, 2016, p. 308.

45. Andrew Ross Sorkin, "What Timothy Geithner Really Thinks," *New York Times*, May 11, 2014. See also President Barack Obama, "Remarks by the President at Signing of Dodd-Frank Wall Street Reform and Consumer Protection Act," Office of the White House Press Secretary, July 21, 2010.

46. Matt Taibbi, "Secret and Lies of the Bailout," *Rolling Stone*, January 4, 2013.

47. "Most people think that the big bank bailout was the $700 billion that the Treasury Department used to save the banks during the financial crash in September of 2008. But this is a long way from the truth because the bailout is still ongoing. The Special Inspector General for TARP summary of the bailout says that the total commitment of government is $16.8 trillion dollars with the $4.6 trillion already paid out." Mike Collins, "The Big Bank Bailout," *Forbes*, July 14, 2015.

48. Taibbi, "Secret and Lies of the Bailout."

49. Donna Brazile, Twitter account, posted March 14, 2014, twitter .com/donnabrazile/status/709582115843805186?lang=en. Brad Woodhouse, Twitter account, posted March 15, 2016, twitter .com/woodhouseb/status/709718180336443392.

50. Bernie Sanders, "Sanders Letter to DNC Chairwoman Debbie Wasserman-Shultz," BernieSanders.com, May 6, 2016.

51. Aaron Blake, "Here Are the Latest, Most Damaging Things in the DNC's Leaked Emails," *Washington Post*, July 24, 2016. See also Michael M. Grynbaum, "CNN Parts Ways with Donna Brazile, a Hillary Clinton Supporter," *New York Times*, October 31, 2016.

52. Donna Brazile, "Inside Hillary Clinton's Takeover of the DNC," *Politico*, November 2, 2017.

53. Reena Flores, "Clinton Piles on Sanders for Stance on Sandy Hook Gun Maker Lawsuit," *CBS News*, April 6, 2016.

54. Marin Cogan, "Drinking Beer and Watching Baseball with Senator Claire McCaskill—the Most Candid Woman in the US Senate," *New York* magazine, August 20, 2015. See also Mark Hensch, "McCaskill: Sanders Has Made Clinton a Better Candidate," *The Hill*, November 9, 2015.

55. Liz Kreutz, "Hillary Clinton Reporters Kept Behind Moving Rope Line at New Hampshire Parade," *ABC News*, July 5, 2015.

56. Sanders, *Our Revolution*, p.122.

57. Ibid.

2. The Campaign, Part 1

1. Anu Narayanswamy, Darla Cameron, and Matea Gold, "Election 2016: Money Raised as of Nov. 28," *Washington Post*, December 9, 2016. See also Simon Head, "The Clinton System," *New York Review of Books*, January 30, 2016.

2. Nicole Gaudiano, "Bernie Sanders Defied Expectations with Long-Shot Presidential Campaign," *USA Today*, July 11, 2016.

3. Representatives Keith Ellison, Tulsi Gabbard, Raul Grijalva, Marcy Kaptur, Peter Welch, Rick Nolan, Colin Peterson, Dan Lipinski, and Alan Grayson.

4. Randi Weingarten and Leo Casey, "Why Hillary Clinton Deserved Labor's Support," *New Labor Forum* 26: 1, 2016, pp. 14–5.

5. Larry Cohen, "We Believe That We Can Win!," *New Labor Forum* 26: 1, 2016, p. 11.

6. Bernie Sanders, "Sanders, Pocan Introduce Legislation to Strengthen Workers' Rights," Bernie Sanders Senate Office (homepage), October 6, 2015.

7. Robert Gebelhoff, "Why Are Unions in the US So Weak?," *Washington Post*, August 1, 2016.

8. "New Release: Union Members—2016," US Bureau of Labor Statistics, January 26, 2017.

9. Megan Dunn and James Walker, "Union Membership in the United States," US Bureau of Labor Statistics, September 2016.

10. RoseAnn DeMoro, "A Vehicle for Change: Nurses Launch National #BernieBus Tour," *Huffington Post*, January 8, 2016.

11. "Ready for Hillary," OpenSecrets.com. See also Leslie Larson, "Hillary Clinton's Campaign Is Absorbing Members of the Ready for Hillary SuperPAC," *Business Insider*, April 1, 2015.

12. Rand Wilson and Dan DiMaggio, "Labor for Bernie Activists Take the Political Revolution into Their Unions," *Labor Notes*, March 17, 2016.

13. Bernie Sanders, "Press Release: Bernie Sanders Earns Endorsement of the United Steelworkers Local 1999," BernieSanders .com, April 19, 2016.

14. Wilson and DiMaggio, "Labor for Bernie Activists Take the Political Revolution into Their Unions."

15. Sam Frizel, "Hillary Clinton Wins Major Endorsement from SEIU," *Time*, November 17, 2015.

16. April McCullum, "Sanders Gets Early Endorsement by VT Teachers," *Burlington Free Press*, June 24, 2015.

17. Adele M. Stan, "AFT's Clinton Endorsement Controversy," *Clarion*, September 2015.

18. Kate Taylor, "Bernie Sanders Urges Cuomo to Raise CUNY Professors' Pay," *New York Times*, December 15, 2015.

19. Mark Landler, *Alter Egos: Hillary Clinton, Barack Obama, and*

the Twilight Struggle Over American Power, New York: Penguin Random House, 2016.

20. Samir Sonti, "Going Back to Class: Why We Need to Make University Free, and How We Can Do It," nonsite.org, May 1, 2013.

21. Kenneth W. Warren and Samir Sonti, "Nobody Is Going to Have to Pay to Go to College," *Chronicle of Higher Education*, December 16, 2015.

22. The Institute of College Access and Success, "Impact of House and Senate Budget Proposals to Freeze the Maximum Pell Grant for 10 Years: Making College Even Less Affordable," March 19, 2015. See also David Reich and Brandon Debot, "House Budget Committee Plan Cuts Pell Grants Deeply, Reducing Access to Higher Education," Center for Budget and Policy Priorities, October 21, 2015.

23. Joseph Stiglitz, "Of the 1%, for the 1%, by the 1%," *Vanity Fair*, March 31, 2011. See also Ryan Teague Beckwith, "Read the Full Text of the Second Democratic Debate," *Time*, November 16, 2015.

24. Sonti, "Going Back to Class: Why We Need to Make University Free, and How We Can Do It."

25. In an interview with CNN, Clinton stated: "I believe that my approach, for example, on college, I call it the New College Compact, because I think everybody should have some skin in the game, including students, who I say should work for part of their education." See Jason Easley, "Hillary Clinton Refuses to Take the Media's Bait and Criticize Bernie Sanders' Positions," Politicususa.com, October 18, 2015.

26. Hillary Clinton, "The New College Compact—Hillary for America," Medium.com.

27. Stacy Cowley, "Many Low-Income Workers Say 'No' to Health Insurance," *New York Times*, October 19, 2015. See also "Key Facts About the Uninsured Population," *The Henry J. Kaiser Family Foundation*, September 29, 2016.

28. Bernie Sanders, S.1782: American Health Security Act, 113th Congress, December 9, 2013.

29. Ezra Klein, "Bernie Sanders Single-Payer Plan Isn't a Plan at All," Vox.com, January 17, 2016. See also Seth Ackerman, "Meet the New Harry and Louise," *Jacobin*, January 25, 2016.

30. Matthew Yglesias, "It's Time to Start Taking Bernie Sanders Seriously," Vox.com, January 18, 2016.

31. Laura Meckler, "Pricetag of Bernie Sanders' Proposal: $18 Trillion," *Wall Street Journal*, September 14, 2015. See also Doug Henwood, "Bernie's New Deal," *Jacobin*, September 17, 2015.

32. Paul Krugman, "Weakened at Bernie's," *New York Times*, January 19, 2016; see also Paul Krugman, "Single-Payer Trouble," *New York Times*, January 28, 2016.

33. Paul Kane, "Pelosi Dismisses Portions of Sanders's Tax and Health-care Agenda: 'It's Not Going to Happen,'" *Washington Post*, January 27, 2016.

34. Nicole Guardiano, "Hillary Clinton, Bernie Sanders Battle Over Meaning of Progressive," *USA Today*, February 4, 2016.

35. Alan Krueger, Austan Goolsbee, Christina Romer, and Laura D'Andrea Tyson, "An Open Letter from Past CEA Chairs to Senator Sanders and Professor Gerald Friedman," February 17, 2016, lettertosanders.wordpress.com/2016/02/17/open-letter-to-senator-sanders-and-professor-gerald-friedman-from-past-cea-chairs.

36. Tami Luhby, "Under Sanders, Income and Jobs Would Soar, Economist Says," *CNN Money*, February 8, 2016. See also Frank Sammartino, Len Burman, Jim Nunns, Joseph Rosenberg, and Jeff Rohaly, "Report: An Analysis of Senator Bernie Sanders' Tax Proposals," Tax Policy Center, March 4, 2016; David Dayen, "Wall Street Journal's Scary Bernie Sanders Price Tag Ignores Health Savings," *Intercept*, September 15, 2015; and Doug Henwood, "Bernie's New Deal," *Jacobin*, January 28, 2016.

37. Greg Kauffman, "Taking on the Dental Crisis: A Q&A with Bernie Sanders," *Nation*, February 27, 2012.

38. Bernie Sanders, "Poverty in America," BernieSanders.com, May 5, 2016.

39. Steve Goldstein, "The Only State Where Less Than Half of All Civilians Work," *MarketWatch*, March 19, 2015. See also Ned Resnikoff, "West Virginia Chemical Spill Leaves 300,000 without Clean Water," MSNBC.com, January 10, 2014. The company that stored the chemicals (regrettably named Freedom Industries) failed to repair holes in the tanks' retaining wall. Those tanks would have failed inspection had environmental regulations on chemical storage been in effect. See "Republican Deregulation Culture to Blame for Water Poisoning West Virginia Chemical Spill," Politicsusa.com, January 13, 2014.

40. Elizabeth Mehren, "Bargain Drug Prices Spark Border Crossings," *Los Angeles Times*, December 4, 2000.

41. Maureen Cosgrove, "Jaunts Across the Border Best Rx for High Drug Prices," *The Pew Charitable Trusts*, September 20, 2000.

42. Bianca Seidman, "Drug Price Increases by 5,000 Percent Overnight," *CBS News*, September 21, 2015.

43. Bernie Sanders, "It's Time to Make College Tuition Free and Debt Free," BernieSanders.com.

44. Max Ehrenfreund, "Bernie Sanders Has a Pretty Revolutionary Idea to Change America's Post Offices," *Washington Post*, October 29, 2015.

45. Jeff Madrick, *Age of Greed: The Triumph of Finance and Decline of America, 1970 to Present*, New York: Knopf, 2011, p. 240. See also Alan Pyke, "The Story Behind Clinton's Jab at Sanders' One Wall Street Vote," *ThinkProgress*, February 5, 2016; Nomi Prins, *All the President's Bankers: The Hidden Alliances That Drive American Power*, New York: Nation Books, 2014, pp. 364–8; and Bob Herbert, "Enron and the Grahams," *New York Times*, January 17, 2002.

46. Mary Williams Walsh, "Hedge Funds Sue Puerto Rico's Governor, Claiming Money Grab," *New York Times*, July 21, 2016.

47. "The Economic Impact of the American Recovery and Reinvestment Act Five Years Later: Final Report to Congress," Executive Office of the President Council of Economic Advisers, February 2014. See also *New York Times* Editorial Board, "What the Stimulus Accomplished," *New York Times*, February 23, 2014.

48. Steve Mufson, "Supreme Court Bars Puerto Rico from Adopting Its Own Bankruptcy Measures," *Washington Post*, June 13, 2016.

49. Larry Elliott, "IMF Tells EU It Must Give Greece Unconditional Debt Relief," *Guardian*, May 23, 2016. See also T. T. Ram Mohan, "How the IMF Bungled the Greek Debt Crisis," *The Wire*, April 8, 2016.

50. Jordain Carney, "Sanders Offers Alternative Puerto Rico Bill," *The Hill*, June 13, 2016. See also Bernie Sanders, "Ending the Humanitarian Crisis in Puerto Rico," BernieSanders.com.

51. Heather Gautney and Franco Barchiesi, "Vieques O Muerte: Transnational Movement and the Politics of Diaspora" (in Italian), *Derive Approdi*, November 2003, pp. 31–36.

52. Bernie Sanders, "Read Bernie Sanders' Speech to AIPAC," Portside.com, March 26, 2016.

53. Zaid Jilani, "Bernie Sanders Won America's Largest Arab Community by Being Open to Them," *Intercept*, March 9, 2016.

54. Clark Mindock, "Who Is Henry Kissinger? Bernie Sanders Attacks Clinton for Asking the Diplomat for Advice as Secretary of State," *International Business Times*, February 11, 2016.

55. Hillary Rodham Clinton, *What Happened*, New York: Simon & Schuster, 2017.

3. The Campaign, Part 2

1. Netroots is an offshoot of DailyKos.com, an online group blog site with a left/progressive readership. The conference attracts

progressive activists from around the country each year, and has featured Democratic Party leaders like Hillary Clinton, Senator Harry Reid, and, in 2015, Bernie Sanders.

2. Chris Moody, "Democrats Lose Control of Campaign Event," CNN.com, July 19, 2015.

3. Martin Pengelly, "O'Malley and Sanders Interrupted by Black Lives Matter in Phoenix," *Guardian*, July 18, 2015.

4. The National Academy for Social Insurance provides a series of reasons why this is the case. Social Security fills in gaps caused by other racial disparities in employment, retirement income, and so on, and is thus a critical source of income, especially for African American populations. See "Social Security and People of Color," National Academy of Social Insurance. This is also the case for women. See "Policy Basics: Top Ten Facts about Social Security," Center for Budget and Policy Priorities, August 12, 2016.

5. Jim Brunner, "Black Lives Matter Protesters Shut Down Bernie Sanders Rally; Later Rally Draws 15,000," *Seattle Times*, August 11, 2016.

6. Adalia Woodbury, "The Real Black Lives Matter Wants to Apologize to Bernie Sanders," Politicususa.com, August 10, 2015.

7. Touré F. Reed, "Why Liberals Separate Race from Class," *Jacobin*, August 22, 2015.

8. Robin D. G. Kelley, "Black Study, Black Struggle," *Boston Review*, March 7, 2016. See also Nancy Fraser's work on second wave feminism's move away from a politics of redistribution toward one of recognition, in Nancy Fraser, "Feminism, Capitalism, and the Cunning of History," *New Left Review* 56, March/April 2009, pp. 97–117; and Cecila Conrad, John Whitehead and Patrick L. Mason (eds.), *African Americans in the US Economy*, New York: Rowman and Littlefield, 2006, pp. 120–4.

9. Dudzic, "The Origin of the Species."

10. As Rustin put it in his address to the 1970 Convention of the Bricklayers, Masons, and Plasterers International Union: "The

fact is that if you are going to deal simultaneously with black rage and white fear, the only group in the nation which has the answer is the organized trade union movement because it says: 'There must be full employment for all who want to work.' If there was full employment, blacks would not be in a rage because they do not have jobs, and whites would not be fearful that they will lose theirs." Bayard Rustin, *Black Rage, White Fear*, Berkeley: University of California Press, 1970.

11. David G. Savage and Paul Richter, "Clinton to Sign Bill Preserving Stiff Crack Rules: Drugs: It would block a move to treat powdered cocaine violations equally. Opponents see a bias, since most of those facing the tougher terms are black," *Los Angeles Times*, October 27, 1995.

12. Adolph Reed, Jr., "Obama No," *Progressive*, April 28, 2008. See also Julie Bosman, "Obama Sharply Assails Absent Black Fathers," *New York Times*, June 16, 2008; and Heather Gautney and Akim Reinhardt, "The Imperial Coin," *Peace and Change* 35: 1, January 2010, pp. 146–63.

13. Adolph Reed, Jr., and Daniel Zamora, "Bernie Sanders and the New Class Politics," *Jacobin*, August 8, 2016; and Reed, "Why Liberals Separate Race from Class."

14. Bernie Sanders, "An Occupying Army," Bernie Sanders Senate Office (homepage), August 19, 2014.

15. Gloria Pazmino, "After Public Anguish, Bronx Councilman Endorses Sanders on Eve of Primary," *Politico*, April 18, 2016.

16. Kevin Gosztola, "Labor Secretary Advised Clinton to Cast Sanders as Candidate of Whites to Turn off Minority Voters," *Commondreams*, October 10, 2016.

17. Luis Gutiérrez, "Sanders Voted with Republicans," *Univision*, February 18, 2016. See also Pema Levy, "Pro-Clinton Latino Leaders Slam Sanders," *Mother Jones*, February 18, 2016.

18. "Grijalva: Gutiérrez's Attacks on Sanders are 'Disingenuous'." *The Hill*, March 1, 2016.

19. AFL-CIO, "Statement of Principles on Immigration and the High-Skill Workforce," AFL-CIO.org. See also Richard Trumka, "Demanding Guestworker Reforms Is Pro-Immigrant," *Huffington Post*, August 5, 2015.

20. Katie Reilly, "Clinton Campaign Considered Tim Cook, Bill Gates, Melinda Gates for VP," *Fortune*, October 18, 2016.

21. Jeff Sommer, "Trump Immigration Crackdown Is Great for Private Prison Stocks," *New York Times*, March 10, 2017.

22. Jon Orlin, "Bernie Sanders Won the Most Votes Ever in a New Hampshire Presidential Primary," *Huffington Post*, February 13, 2016.

23. Jon Ralston, "Harry Reid Delivers for Hillary Clinton," *USA Today*, February 21, 2016.

24. Ashley Rodriguez, "Sanders May Have Lost Nevada, but He Won Over the Crucial Latino Vote," *Quartz*, February 20, 2016. See also Philip Bump, "Did Bernie Sanders Really Just Win the Hispanic Vote in Nevada?," *Washington Post*, February 22, 2016.

25. Jens Manuel Krogstad, "Top Issue for Hispanics? Hint: It's Not Immigration," Pew Research Center, June 2, 2014.

26. According to RealtyTrac, South Carolina has one of the highest rates of foreclosure in the country, with 1 out of every 1,049 households in some stage of foreclosure—a higher incidence than the national average of 1 out of every 1,600 (as of September 2016). See Laura Dunn, "See How States Rank for Foreclosures in September," Bankrate.com. In cities like Charlotte, in 2014, a growing number of lenders were accepting homebuyers with lower credit scores. In 2013, Wells Fargo dropped its credit score for home-purchase loans backed by the Federal Housing Administration from 640 to 600. Bank of America said that it would do the same on a case-by-case basis. See Deon Roberts, "Subprime Lending Beginning to Return to Charlotte," *Charlotte Observer*, March 14, 2014.

27. Amanda Girard, "Video Surfaces of Hillary Clinton Blaming Homeowners for Financial Crisis," *US Uncut*, January 16, 2016.

28. Ben Jealous, "I Endorse Bernie Sanders for President," Bernie-Sanders.com, February 5, 2016.

29. Erica Garner, "Erica Garner's Commercial Endorsing Bernie Sanders for President," Official Website of Erica Garner, February 11, 2016. See also Reena Flores, "Erica Garner's Daughter Criticizes Hillary Clinton After WikiLeaks Emails," CBSNews.com, October 28, 2016.

30. Mark Hensch, "Harry Belafonte Endorses Sanders," *The Hill*, February 11, 2015.

31. Bennett said: "I just think he's an honest guy ... And I think that's what people need to hear, the honest truth ... Not so much about war, but more about improving people, and improving the economy, and just livin' good." Bob Condotta, "Seattle Seahawks' Michael Bennett on Presidential Candidate Bernie Sanders: He's My Pick," *Seattle Times*, December 23, 2015.

32. John Wagner, "Bernie Sanders Hangs with Rapper Killer Mike as He Courts Black Voters in Atlanta," *Washington Post*, November 23, 2015.

33. Daniel Kreps, "Watch Killer Mike Introduce Bernie Sanders with Moving Speech at Atlanta Rally," *Rolling Stone*, November 23, 2015.

34. "Clyburn Endorses Clinton: There Are No Free Lunches, So There Will Be No Free Education," *RealClear Politics*, February 19, 2016.

35. Sean Sullivan, "Jeb Bush: Win Black Voters with Aspiration, Not 'Free Stuff,'" *Washington Post*, September 24, 2015.

36. Milton Friedman, *There's No Such Thing as a Free Lunch: Essays on Public Policy*, Chicago: Open Court Publishing, 1977.

37. Sam Frizell, "Exclusive: College Alumni Raise Doubts About Bernie Sanders Campaign Photo," *Time*, February 12, 2016.

38. Quiana Fulton, "Activist John Lewis Confuses Hillary Clinton

Goldwater Activism for Civil Rights Activism," ReverbPress .com, February 13, 2016.

39. Aaron Guild Sheinin, "John Lewis on Bernie Sanders: 'There's Not Anything Free in America'," *Atlanta Journal Constitution*, February 17, 2016.

40. Ashley Young, "Clyburn: Sanders' Free College Plan Would Hurt Historically Black Colleges," CNN.com, February 22, 2016.

41. Nicole Gaudiano, "Bernie Sanders' Support for Black Colleges Questioned," *USA Today*, February 16, 2016.

42. Bradford Richardson, "Clyburn: Sanders' Plan Would Kill Black Colleges," *The Hill*, February 21, 2016.

43. Cedric Johnson, "Fear and Pandering in the Palmetto State," *Jacobin*, February 29, 2016.

44. Johnson cites exit polls suggesting "that 72 percent of all South Carolina Democrats wanted to continue Obama's policies, and only 18 percent wanted something more liberal than what Obama offered. In the same poll, only 43 percent of black voters identified as liberals." Johnson, "Fear and Pandering in the Palmetto State."

45. Dan Merica, "Clinton Touts Obama in South Carolina, but Promises to Do More for Blacks," CNN.com, November 8, 2015.

46. Gary Langer, Gregory Holyk, and Chad Kiewiet De Jonge, "Black Voters Boost Hillary Clinton to South Carolina Primary Win," *ABC News*, February 27, 2016.

47. Ed Kilgore, "The Secret to Sanders' Shocking Michigan Victory: Breaking the Demographic Mold," *New York* magazine, March 9, 2016.

48. Perry Bacon, "Huge Split Between Older and Younger Blacks in the Democratic Primary," *NBC News*, May 28, 2016.

49. Jonathan Easley, "Poll: Bernie Sanders Country's Most Popular Active Politician," *The Hill*, April 18, 2017.

50. Chris Cillizza, "Hillary Clinton: 18 Million Cracks and the Power of Making History," *Washington Post*, June 13, 2013.

51. Adam Gabbat, "Gloria Steinem: Women Are Supporting Bernie Sanders 'for the Boys,'" *Guardian*, February 6, 2016.

52. Alan Rappeport, "Gloria Steinem and Madeleine Albright Rebuke Young Women Backing Bernie Sanders," *New York Times*, February 7, 2016.

53. David Rieff, "Were Sanctions Right?," *New York Times*, July 23, 2003.

54. Tim Hains, "MSNBC's Joy Reid Horrified by Sanders Supporters 'Throwing Dollar Bills' at Hillary 'As if in a Strip Club,'" *RealClear Politics*, April 17, 2016.

55. Liza Featherstone, "Why This Socialist Feminist Is Not Voting for Hillary," *Nation*, January 5, 2016.

56. Linda Martín Alcoff, Cinzia Arruzza, Tithi Bhattacharya, Nancy Fraser, Barbara Ransby, Keeanga-Yamahtta Taylor, Rasmea Yousef Odeh, Angela Davis, "Women of America: We're Going on Strike. Join Us, So Trump Will See Our Power," *Guardian*, February 6, 2017.

57. Myriam Renaud. "Hillary Clinton's Moral Conflicts on Abortion," *Atlantic*, August 6, 2016.

58. Zaid Jilani and Naomi LaChance, "Hacked Emails Show Hillary Clinton Repeatedly Praised Walmart in Paid Speeches," *Intercept*, October 12, 2016.

59. Communications Workers of America, "Women Beware: Your Jobs, Wages, and Health Are at Risk," *TransPacific Partnership Factsheet*.

60. Walter Benn Michaels, "Let Them Eat Diversity," *Jacobin*, January 2011.

61. Lauren Victoria Burke, "Full Transcript: Hillary Clinton Convo with #BlackLivesMatter," August 18, 2015.

62. Adolph Reed, Jr., "Marx, Race, and Neoliberalism," *New Labor Forum* 22: 1, 2013, 49–57.

63. Ibid.

64. Cedric Johnson: "I am merely pointing out that the reparations

demand exists largely in the realm of the political imaginary, and that in the concrete world of struggle, social democracy and socialism have a demonstrated history of improving the lives of black and other working-class people around the world. The democratic right to organize in the workplace, the Scandinavian social-democratic model, the public works programs of the American New Deal, infrastructural development in Nkrumah's Ghana, Viennese social housing, Cuba's healthcare, education and civil defense systems, Chilean nationalization under Salvador Allende, and so forth." Cedric Johnson, "Reparations Isn't a Political Demand," *Jacobin*, March 7, 2016. See also Adolph Reed, Jr., and Daniel Zamora, "Bernie Sanders and the New Class Politics," *Jacobin*, August 8, 2016; and Heather Gautney and Adolph Reed, Jr., "Bernie Sanders' 'College for All' Plan Is Fair, Smart, and Achievable," *Nation*, December 2, 2015.

65. Cynthia Taylor, *A. Philip Randolph: The Religious Journey of an African American Labor Leader*, New York: New York University Press, 2006, p. 1. See also Judith Stein, "A. Philip Randolph," History.com.

66. Adolph Reed, Jr., "The Black-Labor-Left Alliance in the Neoliberal Age," *New Labor Forum*, February 22, 2016.

67. Adam Johnson, "Cornel West and Chris Hedges: How the Black Elite Betrayed the Civil Rights Tradition," *Alternet*, August 14, 2015.

68. Preston Smith, *Racial Democracy and the Black Metropolis: Housing Policy in Postwar Chicago*, Minneapolis: Minnesota University Press, 2012. See also Adolph Reed, Jr., "The Real Problem with Selma," nonsite.org, January 26, 2015.

69. Some members of the Congressional Black Caucus (CBC) tried to block financial regulation while taking money from the banks. The CBC Foundation, as well as the NAACP, National Urban League, United Negro College Fund, and others, took large sums from Walmart as the company was using race as a marketing tool

(its "urban strategy") and denying workers, a third of whom were African American, a living wage. See E. Tammy Kim, "Black Workers Embody the New Low-Wage Economy," *Al-Jazeera America*, September 12, 2013; James Thindwa, "The Black Political Establishment Should Never Have Given Hillary Clinton a Blank Check," *In These Times*, August 8, 2016; and Anmol Chaddha, "Good for the 'Hood?" *Colorlines*, July 21, 2005.

70. Barbara Ehrenreich, "Maid to Order," *Harper's Magazine*, April 2000, pp. 59–70.

71. Cedric Johnson, "An Open Letter to Ta-Nehisi Coates and the Liberals Who Love Him," *Atlantic*, February 3, 2016.

4. The Convention, the General Election, and Its Aftermath

1. Dan Merica, "Clinton Casts Sanders as 'Pie in the Sky' in Wisconsin," CNN.com, March 29, 2016.

2. Phil Hirschkorn, "America's Last Great Convention: Mondale, Jackson & Hart Dish to Salon About Wild 1984 DNC," *Salon*, February 15, 2015.

3. Eric Levenson, "Barney Frank: Bernie Sanders Has Made 'Serious Mistakes' Since Primary Loss," Boston.com, July 7, 2016.

4. David Weigel, "Obama and Sanders Battle Over TPP and the Democratic Platform," *Washington Post*, June 26, 2016.

5. The precise language in the platform reads, "Democrats are unified in their strong belief that every student should be able to go to college debt-free, and working families should not have to pay any tuition to go to public colleges and universities," Democratic Platform Committee, "The 2016 Democratic Party Platform," Democratic National Committee homepage, July 8–9, 2016.

6. The convention was held at the Wells Fargo Center in Philadelphia. For more on donors, see Matea Gold, "Leaked DNC Emails

Reveal the Inner Workings of the Party's Finance Operation," *Washington Post*, July 24, 2016.

7. Robby Mook, "Berman (2014-4-26)," WikiLeaks.

8. Nicole Gaouette, "The Democrats' Republican Moment," *CNN*, July 30, 2016.

9. Ian Schwartz, "Scarborough: Obama Sounded Like Ronald Reagan at DNC, 'Spoke for My View of America,'" *RealClear Politics*, July 28, 2016.

10. Lee Fang and Zaid Jilani, "Democratic Convention Funded by Republican Donors, Anti-Obamacare Lobbyists," *Intercept*, May 11, 2016.

11. Joe Pappalardo, "Ralph Nader: Sanders Set Clinton Up for 'Political Betrayal,'" Townhall.com, July 18, 2016.

12. Joan Walsh, "Bernie Sanders Is Hurting Himself by Playing the Victim," *Nation*, May 19, 2016.

13. Deidre Walsh, "House Democrats Boo Bernie Sanders in Contentious Meeting," CNN.com, July 6, 2016.

14. Jon Queally, "Backers of Sanders Mobilize to Overthrow DNC Platform's Pro-TPP Stance," *Commondreams*, June 30, 2016.

15. John Cassidy, "Bernie Sanders Gives Hillary Clinton Another Boost," *New Yorker*, July 27, 2016.

16. Susan Davis, "'Dawn of a New Republican Government' Coming in 2017," *NPR Politics*, December 22, 2016.

17. Greg Grandin, "The Road from Serfdom," *Counterpunch*, November 17, 2006.

18. Louis Jacobson, "Bernie Sanders Says He Polls Better Against Donald Trump Than Hillary Clinton Does," *Politifact*, May 29, 2016.

19. The 29 percent figure is based on exit polls. Robert Suro, "Here's What Happened with the Latino Vote," *New York Times*, November 9, 2016.

20. Ben Jacobs, "Hillary Clinton Calls Half of Trump Supporters Bigoted 'Deplorables,'" *Guardian*, September 10, 2016.

21. Dave Jamieson, "Hillary Clinton Secures Organized Labor's Prized Endorsement," *Huffington Post*, June 16, 2016.

22. Philip Bump, "Donald Trump Got Reagan-like Support from Union Households," *Washington Post*, November 10, 2016. See also Kim Moody, "Who Put Trump in the White House?" *Jacobin*, January 11, 2017.

23. Josiah Ryan, "'This Was a Whitelash': Van Jones Takes on the Election Results," CNN.com, November 9, 2016.

24. "Our Revolution Livestream Reaches Over 1 Million People," Our Revolution homepage, December 16, 2016.

25. Jonathan Martin and Maggie Haberman, "Democrats' Leadership Fight Pits West Wing Against Left Wing," *New York Times*, November 22, 2016.

26. Trevor Timm, "Everyone Loves Bernie Sanders, Except, It Seems, the Democratic Party," *Guardian*, March 17, 2017.

27. Jonathan Martin, "Democrats Elect Thomas Perez, Establishment Favorite, as Party Chairman," *New York Times*, February 25, 2017. See also Donald Trump twitter account, posted February 25, 2017 twitter.com/realDonaldTrump/status/835610917568200705.

28. *All In with Chris Hayes*, "Sen. Bernie Sanders on Why Trump Won," MSNBC.com, December 12, 2016.

29. Russell Berman, "Sanders and Kennedy at Liberty, 32 Years Apart," *Atlantic*, September 15, 2015.

30. Jonathan Martin, "Eric Cantor Defeated by David Brat, Tea Party Challenger, in GOP Primary Upset," *New York Times*, June 11, 2014.

31. Gregory Krieg, "It's Official: Clinton Swamps Trump in Popular Vote," CNN.com, December 21, 2016.

32. Zaid Jilani, "Harvey Weinstein Urged Clinton Campaign to Silence Sanders's Black Lives Matter Message," *Intercept*, October 7, 2016. See also Eugene Scott, "Eric Garner's Daughter Blasts Clinton Campaign After WikiLeaks Emails," CNN.com, October

28, 2016; and Andre Stackhouse, "If the DNC Helped Nominate Trump," Medium.com, October 19, 2016.

Conclusion

1. Philip Bump, "Why Putting Coal Miners Out of Work Is a Very Bad Thing to Say in West Virginia," *Washington Post*, May 10, 2016.
2. Robert Suro, "Here's What Happened with the Latino Vote," *New York Times*, November 9, 2016.
3. Manuel Castells, *The Power of Identity: The Information Age: Economy, Society, and Culture*, Volume 2, West Sussex: Wiley-Blackwell, 1997, p. 79.
4. Chris McGreal, "How Hosni Mubarak Misread His Military Men," *Guardian*, February 12, 2011.
5. Jacob Rosdahl and Lene Frøslev, "Tunisian Trade Unions Receive Nobel Peace Prize 2015," International Trade Union Confederation (homepage), October 15, 2015. See also Andy Kroll, Nick Baumann, and Siddhartha Mahanta, "What's Happening in Wisconsin Explained," *Mother Jones*, March 17, 2011; and Andy Kroll, "Occupy Wall Street, Powered by Big Labor," *Mother Jones*, October 5, 2011.
6. Alessandro Bessi and Emilio Ferrara, "Social Bots Distort the 2016 US Presidential Election Online Discussion," *First Monday* 21, no. 11, November 7, 2016.
7. Heather Gautney, *Protest and Organization in the Alter-Globalization Era*, New York: Palgrave, 2010.
8. Kim Moody, "Who Put Trump in the White House?," *Jacobin*, November 11, 2017.
9. Harry Davies and Danny Yadron, "How Facebook Tracks and Profits from Voters in a $10bn US Election," *Guardian*, January 28, 2016.

10. Collier Meyerson, "Nina Turner: It Is Not Our Job to Fit Into the Democratic Establishment," *Nation*, June 30, 2017.

11. Ibid.

12. "Senate Democrats Lay Out Key Principles for Tax Reform" (press release), Office of Senator Diane Feinstein, August, 1, 2017.

Index

abortion rights ix, 92
Access Hollywood tapes 117
Adelson, Sheldon 18
Affordable Care Act 57
Afghanistan 29
AFL-CIO 50, 78, 118
Age of Inequality 19–26
Airline Deregulation Act 21
Al Jazeera 110
Alabama 9
Albright, Madeleine 90
Allen, John 111
Amalgamated Transit Union xv, 49
American Association for the
    Advancement of Science 5
American Association of Retired
    Persons 25
American Civil Liberties Union
    (ACLU) 139
American Federation of State,
    County, and Municipal
    Employees 49–50, 106
American Federation of Teachers
    45, 49, 50, 51, 108
American Israel Public Affairs
    Committee (AIPAC) 66

American Postal Workers Union xv,
    49, 63
American Sociological Association 5
anticommunism 23
antidiscrimination x
anti-establishment forces 117
    rise of 101
antiracism 71–7
antiracist activists 71–3
antiwar activism 4
Arab American News 67
Arab Spring 129, 130
austerity politics 21

banks 150n44
    bailouts 33, 63, 150n47
Belafonte, Harry 84
Bell, William 137
benefits, eligibility requirements 3
Benghazi 5
Bennett, Michael 84
Bernanke, Ben 34
Bernie Buses 49
bias, challenging 94–8
big government 21, 23
Big Pharma 61–2

Bipartisan Commission on
    Entitlement and Tax Reform 25
Birmingham, Alabama 137
Black Lives Matter 71–3
black voters 75, 85, 87–9, 161n4
black youth unemployment 73
Blair, Tony 26
Bloomberg, Michael 111
Booker, Corey 140
Bowen, Barbara 51
Brat, David 125
Brazile, Donna 36
Briggs, Michael 84, 124
budget deficit 21
Burger King 79
Bush, George W. xvii, 29
Bush, Jeb 85
Business Roundtable 20, 48

California 35
California, University of 50
A Call to Economic Arms (Tsongas)
    24
campaign finance 42–5, 93
Canada 61
Cantor, Eric 125
capitalism 128
Carter, Jimmy 21–2, 26, 33, 101
Castro, Julian 77
Central America Free Trade
    Agreement 79
Charleston 82
Chavez-Thompson, Linda 26
China 52
Chronicle of Higher Education 54
Citicorp 33
Citizens United 4, 18, 31, 42–3
City University of New York
    (CUNY) 51, 55
class antagonisms 118
class politics 95
class war 20
climate change 42

Clinton, Bill x, xviii, 24–5, 67, 102
    budget, 1993 25–6
    financial liberalization 33
    presidency 26–9, 32, 33, 64
    welfare reform agenda 26
Clinton, Hillary
    appeal to identity politics 9
    appeals to feminism 129
    attacks BS's CFMA support 63–4
    basket of deplorables xviii
    BS endorsement of 101, 102, 112
    on BS's agenda 68–9
    defeat by Trump 117–9, 123,
        125–6
    Democratic Party primary, 2008
        90
    and discrimination 94–5
    electoral defeat 2
    email scandal 118
    entitlement x
    as First Lady 27–8
    foreign policy 66–8
    health care policy 57
    higher education policy 56, 93,
        107, 153n25
    immigration policy 77
    low popularity x, 19
    minimum wage policy 47, 69, 92,
        105, 108–9
    neoliberalism 126
    New College Compact 56, 153n25
    nomination seen as inevitable ix–x
    patronage networks 43
    platform negotiations 104, 105
    platform representatives 103, 109
    popularity x, 19, 37, 99
    popularity among black voters 89
    on predatory lending 83
    problems 1
    qualifications as candidate x
    and racism 74
    running mate 78
    status 128–9

supporters x
ties to Kissinger 67–8
trade policy 51–2, 93, 106
union endorsement of 45–6, 50
Unity Amendment 109
visit to New York 76
What Happened 68–9
Clinton nomination campaign xx, 88
    campaign finance 43, 44–5, 93
    enthusiasm xx–xxi
    gender politics 89–94
    ignorance of the needs of the
        working class 10
    and inequality 128–9
    Nevada victory 80–1
    New York victory 99
    offers x–xi
    organizational chart 37
    promises 100–1
    South Carolina 81, 84–6
    South Carolina victory 86–7
    strategic flaws 118
    superdelegate lead 45
    victory 99–100, 125
Clintonism x
Clyburn, James 84–5, 86
Coalition of Immokalee Workers
    79–80
Cohen, Larry 23, 45–6, 47, 49
collectivism 23
college education, costs 53–5
College for All Act 55, 63
Comey, James 125–6
Commodities Futures Modernization
    Act 63–4
Communications Workers of
    America 45, 48–9
community health centers 60
Concord Coalition, the 25
Congressional Black Caucus 85, 97,
    163–4n69
Congressional Progressive Caucus
    32

Coons, Chris 6
corporate Democrats xiv
corporate feminism 91–2
corporate taxation 15
Council of Economic Advisers 58
credit agencies 63
criminal justice policy 73
Culinary Workers Union 81
Cummings, Elijah 105, 113–4
Cuomo, Andrew 51

Dakota Access pipeline 76
Dawson, Rosario 49
Dean, Howard 111
Deans, Dottie 116
Dearborn, Michigan 67
Debs, Eugene 14, 16–7
debt 29
de-commodification 141
Democracy Daily 82
Democracy for America 35
Democratic Leadership Council 26
Democratic liberalism 143–4n1
Democratic National Committee 36,
    101, 110, 111, 120
    national platform drafting process
        101–9
    Platform Drafting Committee 67,
        101–4, 113
    Rules Committee 103
    Unity Reform Commission 103
Democratic National Convention
    100, 101, 103, 110–6
Democratic neoliberalism xviii, xix,
    xxi–xxii, 143–4n1
Democratic Party
    abandons South 9
    and the Age of Inequality 19–26
    BS and 31–9
    BS on 32
    class interests 41
    class program 26–7
    under Clinton 26–9

dominant wing ix–x, xi
electoral coalition xx
electoral losses, 2014 35
fiscal responsibility strategy 23–4
hostility to BS 36–7
leadership 36, 41
lip service 18–9
loss of influence 1
losses 1, 35
move rightward xix–xx
national platform 101, 101–9
neoliberal presumptions xi
New Economy 10
under the Trump presidency
    139–40
welfare ideology 26
and working-class insecurity
    xviii
Democratic Party Jefferson-Jackson
    dinner 82
democratic socialism 7, 14–6, 41–2
DeMoro, RoseAnn 49
dental care, hidden crisis of 60
DeVos, Betsy 139
Dewitt, Donna xiv
digital following 44
Dimon, Jamie 63
Dingell, Debbie 120
Discourse 143–4n1
discrimination 94–8
diversity x, 128–9
Dodd-Frank act 34
door-knocking outreach xii
DREAM Act 79
drug industry 61–2
Dudzic, Mark xxi–xxii, 22–3
Dukakis, Michael 26
Duncan, Arne 30

education reform 30
Edwards, Edwin 13
egalitarianism 15
Ehrenreich, Barbara 97

electoral action xii–xiii
electoral campaigns 132–5
Ellison, Keith 67, 120–1
Emanuel AME Church massacre
    81, 82
Enron loophole, the 64
environmental regulation 42
establishment, the 100
European socialism 7–8
exit polls 89, 161n44

Facebook 44, 129–30, 132, 134
Fairfax, Virginia 61
Fallon, Brian 111
Farrakhan, Louis 121
Featherstone, Liza 91
federal government, reactionaries
    control of xviii–xix
Federal Reserve, the 63
    audit 34
Feldstein, Martin 25
feminism 94, 129, 157n8
    corporate 91–2
    glass ceiling 97
    lean-in 91, 91–2
    socialist 91
Ferrisburgh, Vermont 9
financial liberalization 28–9, 33–4,
    100
financial markets
    deregulation 28–9, 33, 62–3
    re-regulation 62–6
financial transactions tax 63
Florida Tomato Growers Exchange
    79
Folsom Elementary, South Hero
    6–7, 8
Foner, Eric 15–7
Fordham University 3
foreclosure rates 82, 159n26
Foreign Policy 52
foreign policy 66–8
Frank, Barney 102

Franken, Al 6
free market policy 96
free trade 28–9, 37, 49, 51–2, 100, 106, 113, 117, 122, 136
free trade agreements 32, 42, 46, 52, 79, 93
Freedom Industries 155n39
Friedman, Milton 20, 21, 85

Gardner, Erica 83–4
Gates, Bill 78
Gautney, Heather
  academic career 2, 9
  Democratic National Convention 110
  fellowship with Sanders 2, 3–9
  and Higher Ed for Bernie campaign 74–5
  higher education 55
  as platform representative 103, 104–5, 106–7, 109
  Washington Post essay 9–10
Gaza 66
gender 10
gender inequality 77, 128, 137
gender politics 89–94, 94, 95, 98
Georgetown University 16
Georgia 9
Gingrich Revolution, the 27
Glass-Steagall Act 32–3, 63
global competitiveness 56
globalization 62, 118
Glover, Danny 84
Goldwater, Barry 85
Gore, Al xvii
Government Accountability Office 3
government regulation 15
government spending 21
Gramm, Phil 64
Grandin, Greg 68
Grassley, Chuck 78
grassroots organizing 129–32
Great Recession of 2007 27, 29, 30

Greece 65
Greenspan, Alan 3, 17–8, 24
Grijalva, Raúl 78–9
guest workers 78
Gunnels, Warren 67–8, 86
Gutiérrez, Luis 77–9
Gutman, Huck 5–6, 9

Harris, Kamala 140
Harris, Maya 105
Hartmann, Thom 3
Harvard-Harris poll 89
Hayek, Friedrich von 117
health care, and social class 31, 60–1
health care policy 57–62
Henwood, Doug 58
Herbert, Bob 64
Heritage Foundation 48
Higher Ed for Bernie 74–5, 135
higher education grants 28, 54
higher education policy 53–6, 86, 93, 107–8, 153n25
Hightower, Jim 106, 112
Hightower Amendment, the 106
Hillary Victory Fund 93
Hilton DoubleTree, Orlando 101–9
historically black colleges and universities 86
House Committee on Financial Services 17–8
House of Representatives 32
human capital 56
Humphrey-Hawkins bill 20
Hurricane Katrina 29

identity politics 9–10, 120–1
Illinois 35
immigrant laborers 79–80
immigration policy 42, 77–81
Immokalee 79–80
Indiana 115
Indianapolis, Carrier plant 52
industrial Keynesianism 15

inequality x, 3–4, 77, 127–9, 137
inflation 21
interest rate ceilings 33
International Brotherhood of
    Electrical Workers 50
International Business Times 68
International Longshore and
    Warehouse Union xv
International Longshoremen's
    Association 49
International Monetary Fund 4, 65
investor class, the xvii, xviii
Iowa 35, 80, 88, 133
Iraq War 29, 66
Israel 66–7

Jackson, Jesse 32, 101
Jealous, Ben 83, 106
John Birch Society, the 20
Johnson, Cedric 87, 97–8, 161n44,
    163n64
Johnson, Lyndon B. 16
Jones, Chuck 50
Julian, Dolores 77–9

Kelley, Robin 73
Kennedy, Ted 101, 124
Kenosha County, Wisconsin 122
Kerrey, Bob 25
Kerry, John xvii
Keynesianism 15, 19, 20–1, 64
Keystone XL 76
Kilborn, Peter T. 23–4
Kissinger, Henry 67–8
Klein, Ezra 58
Klein, Naomi 49
Koch, Fred 20
Koch Brothers 18, 20, 30
Krugman, Paul 58, 59

Labor, Department of 47–8
Labor for Bernie xi, xii, 49, 135
Labor for Our Revolution 138

Labor Party xiii–xv
labor regulation 42
Lafer, Gordon 20
Lake Champlain 38
Landers, Mark 53
Latino voters 75, 77
lean-in feminism 91, 91–2
Lee, Spike 84
Lew, Jack 65
Lewis, John 85–6
liberalism xx, 143–4n1
Liberty University 124–5
Livestream 44
Lizard's Thicket 87–8
Long, Huey 13–4
Louisiana 82

McAlevey, Jane 144n2
McCaskill, Claire 36–7
McDowell County, West Virginia
    60–1
Maine 137
Mandela, Nelson 133
manufacturing jobs 27
market economy, the 15, 19–20
Markey, Ed 6
mass consistency 133
mass constituency, building 129–32
Mazzocchi, Anthony xviii
media, the
    attacks on BS 36–7
    writes BS off 38
Medicaid 123, 137, 140
Medicare 18, 24, 69, 123, 136, 140
Medicare for All 37, 69, 93, 136, 140
Merkley, Jeff 45
Michaels, Walter Benn 93–4
Michigan 89, 115, 117, 120
Middle East, the 67
midterm elections, 1994 27
millennial voters 44, 90, 134
Mills, C. Wright 4
Milwaukee debate 67–8

minimum wage 47, 68–9, 79, 92, 105, 108–9
Mississippi 9
mobilization xii, xix
Mondale, Walter 24, 26, 32
Moody, Kim 131
Mook, Robby 110, 111
Moore, Lawrence 88
movement-building xii–xiii, 132–5
moveon.org 35

Nader, Ralph xvii, 35, 112
NASDAQ headquarters 83
Nation 16, 91, 104–5, 112, 137
National Academy for Social Insurance 157n4
National Association for the Advancement of Colored People (NAACP) 83, 106
National Association of Manufacturers 20
National Education Association 50
National Labor Relations Board 46
National Nurses United 48–9
National Nurses United for Patient Protection 49
National Nurses United/California Nurses Association xv
National Review 14–5
Native Americans 76
NBC News 89
neofascism 138
neoliberalism 21–4, 126
    definition 22–3
    Democratic xviii, xix, xxi–xxii
    presumptions xi
neopopulism 17
Netanyahu, Benjamin 66
Netroots 71, 157n1
Netroots Nation conference 71–3
Nevada 77, 77–81
New College Compact 153n25
New Deal, the 16

New Democrats 26–7, 31, 32–3
New Economy 10
New Hampshire 35, 50, 80–1, 83, 88, 115, 133
New Labour 26
New York 36, 76–7, 99
New York Daily News 36
New York Review of Books 43
New York Times 18, 23–4, 32, 51, 121
No Child Left Behind 29
North American Free Trade Agreement 4, 32, 79
Nussbaum, Karen 9

Obama, Barack x, xviii, xx, xxi, 33–4, 53, 74, 96, 114, 161n44
    achievements 31
    Democratic National Convention speech 111, 113
    devotion to 87
    electoral popularity 119
    postfinancial crisis recovery 64
    presidency 29–31
    as socialist 30
    trade policy 51, 52
    and the unions 47
    white working-class support 145n6
Obama, Michelle 111
Obamacare 31, 69, 93, 120, 139
Occupy Wall Street 4, 130, 131
O'Donnell, Lawrence 76
Ohio 117
Olin, John M. 20
O'Malley, Martin 69, 74, 111
organizing approach xiii
Orlando, Hilton DoubleTree 101–9
Our Revolution 49, 135, 135–8
outsourcing 22, 78, 93, 125

patronage networks 43
payday loans 82–3
Pell Grants 54

Pelosi, Nancy 58
People for Bernie 135
Peoples' Summit, The 49
Perez, Tom 77, 120–1
Perot, Ross 24
Peters, Gary 120
Peterson, Pete 24, 25
pharmaceutical industry 61–2
Phillips, Abby 91
Piketty, Thomas 15
Podesta, John 104
police, militarization of 75, 81
political alienation 39
political alliance xix
political economy 97–8, 128
political revolution 8–9, 10, 15
Politt, Katha 26, 91
polls xvi, 18–9
postfinancial crisis recovery 64
poverty 3–4, 27, 60, 60–1, 76, 97–8
predatory lending 82–3
presidential election, 1984 23–4
presidential election, 1992 24–5
presidential election, 2004 xvii
presidential election, 2016 35, 116–9
primaries 36, 90, 125
Priorities USA Action 45
prison inmate increase 28
privatization 22, 25, 30, 54, 117
process, valued over goals 143–4n1
Progressive Democrats 35
Progressive Democrats of America 35
public education, corporate attack on x
public goods 141
public investment 15
public sector investment 30
public–private partnerships 56, 122
Puerto Rico 64–6, 76
Putin, Vladimir 125–6, 138

Quinn, Pat xix–xx

race and racism xvi, 27–8, 29–30, 71–7, 94, 95, 116, 128, 137
  inequality 10, 97–8
  Nevada 77–81
  South Carolina 81–9
  Trump voters 126, 145n6
racial profiling 74, 81
racialization 95
Rand, Ayn 117
Randolph, A. Philip 16, 73, 96, 98
Rauner, Bruce xx
reactionaries, control of federal government xviii–xix
Ready for Hillary 49
Ready for Warren 35
Reagan, Ronald 3, 17, 22–4, 26, 27, 96
recognition, politics of 73
Reed, Adolph, Jr. 22–3, 74, 74–5, 87, 88, 97
Reed, Touré 72–3, 75
reforms 13–4
refugees 78–9
Regulation Q interest rates 21–2
Reid, Harry 80–1
Reid, Joy 90–1
reproductive rights ix, 92
Republican Party ix, xxi, 100
  BS on 32
  BS's work with 78
  misogyny x–xi
  shift to the Right 68
Richmond, Cedric 86
rightwing hooliganism 10
Rockefeller, John D. 14
Roosevelt, Franklin D. 16, 32–3
Russia 126, 138
Rustin, Bayard 73, 156n10
Ryan, Paul 116–7

Sandberg, Sheryl 91–2
Sanders, Bernie
  age 37

antagonism to Democrats 32
authors fellowship with 2, 3–9
campaign against Wall Street
    deregulation 4
campaign launch speech 38–9
Clinton on agenda 68–9
commitment to working class 41
concedes nomination 115–6
decision to run as a Democrat
    34–7
Democratic National Convention
    speech 111–2
and the Democratic Party 31–9
democratic socialism 41–2
democratic socialism speech 16
digital following 44
empathy 78–9
endorsement of Clinton 101, 102,
    112
entry into the 2016 primary 31
expectation of xi–xii
financial markets re-regulation
    policy 62–6
foreign policy 66–8
goal 15–6
green agenda 117
health care policy 57–62
higher education policy 55, 86,
    93, 107
House of Representatives service
    32
immigration policy 77–81
issue positions 8
Liberty University speech 124–5
media attacks 36–7
Medicare for All 37, 69, 93, 136,
    140
minimum wage policy 69, 79, 92
Netroots Nation conference
    apearance 71–3
New Deal 60
online presence 130
platform negotiations 103, 105

platform representatives 103
policy proposals 41–2
political agenda 8
political capital 113
political identity 13–7, 31–2
popularity 99, 132
popularity among black voters 89
populism 125
program 15–7
social democratic policies 7–9
socialism 14–6, 18
southern swing 9
success xv, 1–2, 141
support for CFMA 63–4
supporters commitment 100
tax policy 58–9
trade policy 52, 106
after Trump victory 120–6
union support xv
Unity Tour 121–2
visit to New York 76–7
visits Puerto Rico 65, 76
Wall Street greed denunciations
    17–8
Wall Street reform 108
wins second term as US Senator 7
work with Republicans 78
Sanders, Jane 135–6
Sanders, Larry 115
Sanders Institute, the 135–6
Sanders nomination campaign xi–xii
antiracism 71–7
building on xviii–xix
campaign finance 42–5
campaign office 38
class interests 47
decision to run as a Democrat
    34–7
defeat 99–100
Democratic hostility to 36–7
democratic socialism 41–2
and discrimination 94–8
donations 38

focus xi
fund-raising 37, 43, 44
gender politics 90–4
goal 132–3
health care policy debate 58
interviews 37
launch 38–9
lessons 127–35
movement-building 133–5
Nevada 77–81
Nevada defeat 80–1
New York defeat 99
political agenda 8
significance of 100–1
South Carolina 81–9
South Carolina defeat 86–9
success xv–xvi, 141
union endorsements 48–51
and the unions 45–51
use of new media 44
Saunders, Lee 106
Savage, Luke 143–4n1
Savings and Loans 17, 33
Scaife, Richard Mellon 20
Scarborough, Joe 111
Schumer, Chuck 120, 139–40
scientific fact, politics trumps 5
Scott, Walter, police murder of 81
Seattle 72
Second Bill of Rights 16
Service Employees International
    Union 6, 50
Sessions, Jeff 139
sexism xvi, 91, 95, 128
silent majority, the 10
social class 9–10
    antagonisms 118
    Democratic Party and 26–7
    and health care 60–1
    Sanders campaign interests 47
social democracy 7–9, 19, 25–6
social inequality 17, 127–9
social media 44, 129–32, 134

social movements 132–5
social safety nets 15
Social Security 3, 18, 24, 123, 140,
    157n4
Social Security Works 72
social welfare system 27–8
socialism 7–8, 14–6, 18, 41–2
socialist feminism 91
Socialist Party 14
Sonti, Samir 54, 56
South Carolina 9, 50, 77, 81–9,
    159n26, 161n44
South Carolina AFL-CIO xiv
South Carolina Labor Party xiii–xiv
South Carolina, University of 9
South Hero 6–7, 8
Southern California, University of
    131
Southern Christian Leadership
    Conference Gala, 57th National
    Convention 82
southern swing 9
Stabenow, Debbie 120
state divestment 22
Steele, Michael 111
Stein, Judith 19
subprime mortgages 82, 159n26
Super PACs 43, 44, 45, 49
Supreme Court 64
    Citizens United decision 42–3

tax policy 42, 58–9
Taylor, D. 81
Tea Party, the 4, 30, 125, 133, 138
television advertising 131, 134
Temporary Assistance for Needy
    Families 27
Texas 35, 112
Thatcher, Margaret 23, 26
The Other Guy Is Worse ix, x, xi,
    xix, xx
Time magazine 85
top 1 percent, the 3, 6, 22, 29, 92, 123

Torres, Ritchie 76–7
trade policy 51–2, 93, 105–7, 113–4
Trans-Pacific Partnership 30, 47,
    51–2, 93, 105–7, 113–4, 136
    Investor-State Dispute Settlement
        system 53
Troubled Assets Relief Program 34,
    150n47
Trumka, Richard 50, 118
Trump, Donald
    electoral victory xvii, xx, xxi, 2,
        116–9, 125–6, 129
    immigration policy 80
    lack of popularity 119
    misogyny 117, 139
    Muslim ban 139
    nomination xviii
    opposition to 139
    presidency xvi, 120–6, 138–41
    rightwing hooliganism 10
    and the silent majority 10
    trade policy 106
    white working-class support
        145n6
    xenophobia 122
Trump voters xviii, xix, 145n6
Trumpism 126
Tsongas, Paul 24
Tunisia 130
Turner, Nina 83, 137
Twitter 44, 129–30

unemployment 21, 28, 31, 97–8
    black youth 73
unions xix–xx, 6, 31, 78
    BS and xv, 45–51
    collective bargaining 48
    endorsement of BS 48–51
    endorsement of Clinton 45–6,
        50
    membership decline 47–8
    role in US politics 47–8
Unite HERE! 50

United Automobile Workers Local
    72 122
United Electrical, Radio, and
    Machine Workers of America
    xv, 49
United Kingdom, Winter of
    Discontent 23
United Steelworkers Local 1999 50
Unity Amendment 109
US Bureau of Labor Statistics 47–8
US Chambers of Commerce 20
US Navy 65–6
USA Today 81

Vermont 50, 60, 88, 116
Vermont-Maine-New Hampshire
    breakfast 111
Virginia 125
Volcker Shock, the 21
voter disenchantment 100
voter files 36
voting rights 75

Wall Street xvii, 17–8
    bailout 30, 34, 63, 78, 118
    deregulation 4
    re-regulation 29, 62–6, 108
Wall Street Journal 58
Walmart 92, 164n69
Walsh, Joan 91, 112
Walton, Alice 93
Warren, Elizabeth 35, 120, 140
Warren, Kenneth 54
Washington Post 9–10, 46, 91
Wasserman Schultz, Debbie 36
wealth
    distribution 3, 18–9
    inequality 29, 31, 39
    redistribution 13, 31
Weingarten, Randi 45, 108, 120
welfare queens 3, 27, 95
welfare reform 32
West, Cornel 17, 74, 96–7, 109, 112

West Virginia 117, 128, 155n39
WikiLeaks 36, 77, 110
Wisconsin 117, 130
woman vote x–xi, 90, 134
Women, Infants, and Children
   (WIC) program 92
women's political concerns ix
Woodfin, Randall 137
Woodhouse, Brad 36
Workfare 27
Working America 9
working class
   BS's commitment to 41
   Clinton's ignorance of the needs
      of 10
   definition xiii
   engagement with 138

   fundamental concerns xiv–xv,
      xxi
   insecurity xviii
   support of Trump 145n6
   voter participation 131
Workplace Democracy Act 46
World Social Forum 131
World Trade Organization 4
Wounded Knee Massacre 76
Wriston, Walter 33

Yakima, Washington 76
Yglesias, Matt 58

Zogby, James 67
Zuckerberg, Mark 78, 125
Zweig, Michael xiii